DISCARD

THE RING AND THE BOOK

A Study of
BROWNING'S
THE RING AND
THE BOOK

By *James Cassidy*
(E. M. Story)

HASKELL HOUSE PUBLISHERS Ltd.
Publishers of Scarce Scholarly Books
NEW YORK, N.Y. 10012
1971

First Published 1924

HASKELL HOUSE PUBLISHERS Ltd.
Publishers of Scarce Scholarly Books
280 LAFAYETTE STREET
NEW YORK. N. Y. 10012

Library of Congress Catalog Card Number: 74-117581

Standard Book Number 8383-1014-1

Printed in the United States of America

I GRATEFULLY DEDICATE THIS STUDY
TO MY DEAR FRIEND,
MARIE VINCE,
BUT FOR WHOSE UNFAILING SYMPATHY
AND PERSONAL HELP IT WOULD
CERTAINLY NOT HAVE BEEN
PUBLISHED

E.M.S., 1924.

CONTENTS

CONTENTS

BOOK No. I.

"THE RING AND THE BOOK"

BOOK No. I

"THE RING AND THE BOOK"

BOOK No. I

My Dear Friend,

I WONDER if you have ever read the story of
" The Ring and The Book," or, reading it, if you
have been by turns, Robert Browning; Pompilia;
Guido ; Caponsacchi ; even old Pietro and Violante,
and, perhaps, greatest of all, Pope Innocent XII. Have
you ever thought of yourself as " Half-London,"
or even" Half-Edinburgh," " Half-Oxford," " Half-
Cambridge," "Half-Cape Town," "Half-New York"?
If you did so think, it was quite easy, later, to imagine
yourself as " The Other Half."

If kind of heart you would certainly shun becoming
" The Third Thing," that satirical, sceptical, unkindly
" Third," that sits upon the fence, and watches " which
way the cat jumps," and then pronounces " Anyone
might have known as much." You scarce could think of
yourself as " Tertium Quid," and as for me, I am loth
to allot you such a rôle. In due time will you claim
it for the nonce and so, perchance, save me the in-
sidious task ! For a brief period let me urge you to
abdicate your own individuality in favour of that of
Robert Browning. Mrs. Browning has been dead for
but a short time and from your watchchain hangs a
ring of Etruscan shape and style but made in Rome,
by a man world-famous in his Jeweller's Art, " Castel-
lani." On the ring are engraved the letters *A.E.I.*,
probably Greek for " Evermore." On many a day,
before you had attached it to your chain, you had
bent to admire its workmanship of delicate beauty

on the hand of her who had been to you " all a wonder and a wild desire." In together discussing the workmanship of the ring, you had likely spoken of the alloy used by the device of the craftsman to enable him to work the soft gold. The alloy melted with the gold, imparted the necessary hardness to enable it to bear the hammer and the file, and the tools of the craftsman. The removal of the alloy, after the working of the gold, was by means of " Just a spirt of the proper fiery acid o'er its face," which caused it " to fly off in fume." And

> " Self-sufficient now, the shape remains,
> The rondure brave, the lilied loveliness,
> Gold as it was, is, shall be evermore."

You now see in that ring, you have in days gone looked at together, a symbol, many symbols of things signified.

Your thoughts are busy with the ring maybe and with her memory, on whose beloved finger it had erstwhile shone. You arrive in due time at the Square, Piazza di San Lorenzo, Florence, and find yourself in the midst of the market barrows, and the market folk, many of whom you know by sight, and most of whom know you even better. You who are interested, intensely interested, in all human life, stand still and watch the stall-keepers as they offer their wares—such a collection, almost as varied as the wants of human nature.—The Square is " crammed with booths, buzzing and blaze, noontime and market-time." Under the shadow of a statue of a Medici, commonly known as " John of the Black Bands," are ranged books, right and left. *That* you immediately notice, and pull out one from the rest, and glancing at the letter-back shout " Stall," and when the owner comes you ask the price. He tells you " Eightpence " ; if you had offered him half the amount he would not have refused a sale, but you are too deeply impressed with your find, and throw down the money, and pass on.

" You toss and take again—the book,
    Small-quarto size, part print, part manuscript
    A book in shape, but really pure, crude fact
    Secreted from man's life when heart beats hard,
    And brains high-blooded, tricked two centuries since."

Your eager hands turn the ancient pages ; you stand awhile by the low railing, close to the statue, and read on and on.   Then the life and the movement, surging round you, cause you to saunter forth, from the shadow of the sheltering statue, through the familiar streets, but you still read on, from written title page to written index, till by the time you stand at home again, you have read the entire contents, " mastered them, know the whole truth, gathered together, bound up in the book."   You turn again to the title page ; you translate it thus :

                " A Roman Murder Case
        Position of the entire criminal cause
        Of Guido Franceschini, nobleman,
        With certain Four, the cutthroats in his pay,
        Tried all five, and found guilty and put to death
        By heading or hanging, as befitted ranks,
        At Rome on February Twenty-Two
        Since Our Salvation Sixteen Ninety Eight :
        Wherein it is disputed if, and when,
        Husbands may kill adulterous wives, yet scape
        The customary forfeit."

That, you discover, is what this old, square yellow book is all about,
    The thought occurs to you that as the jeweller, Castellani, of old Rome, mixed his soft gold with alloy, that he might harden it and render it fit to work, and so produce his thing of loveliness, so you, taking these hard crude facts set down in this ancient book, will so fuse them with your own personality, permitting the warm sun of your fancy to play on them, and so transmute them from the cold facts of days long gone, to hot, pulsating life, until they become more alive to-day,

than when the contemporary chroniclers set down the record.

> As the great Elisha of old times Stretched himself on the corpse dead on the Couch and put his mouth upon its mouth and his eyes upon its eyes, his hands upon its hands and the flesh waxed warm, and eventually the eyes opened,

So you by a special gift, an art of arts, having more insight and more outsight and much more will than have your friends, send forth half your soul into these dry facts, and behold the dead bones live, and there step out from the charnel house of the past, the living, breathing, men and women—Guido ; Caponsacchi ; Pompilia ; Pietro ; Violante and the Pope. The little yellow book is *alive*, breathing, throbbing, pulsating with a fulness of life. There is *no Past* ; it is all *Now*. and you are the centre of every movement, the occasion or the recipient of every thrill, the All-seeing, All-feeling Artist, the discoverer of Truth. . . . Truth's heart and soul, the Creator. You put the book away for the time, but not its contents. You talk of them with your friends. One day, when a dozen friends are assembled, you tell a simple incident, and you ask each in turn to tell it again, as you told it, and to interpret it. Each teller varies it ; each finds his own interpretation. You laugh, triumphantly as you think of your quarto.

Presently you remove from Casa Guidi, where *she* had been with you, and being a very Englishman, you return to the hub of the universe, good old London—and in Warwick Crescent, with the old, familiar Convent bookcase,[1] and the things she looked upon and liked, and talked about, you pull out from its place the little book, to see how, after the lapse of time and after this change of place, it strikes you ! You turn its leaves, and though Florence has yielded to London, you find

---

[1] This bookcase is now in possession of Mrs. Webb of Drayton Gardens, London, W. It is 12ft. high by 7ft. broad—fine old carved oak.

its influence strong, even stronger, and instead of you
holding the book, it holds you, and

> " A spirit laughs and leaps through every limb
> And lights your eye and lifts you by the hair,
> Letting you have your will again with these,"

until no mere names of strangers are before you, but
those of people whom you know, who step out, and bare
their hearts to you at your bidding. Speedily your
room fills and the old gargoyles on the oak bookcase
wink and laugh and shake their heads and share the
secrets that are open to you by them of the book.

One of the characters standing before you is Guido
Franceschini himself ; he comes of an ancient house,
now fallen on poverty. His nose is beaked, his hair
and bushy beard are black, he is thin and pallid, short
but strong. Though fifty years old he has been married
but four years. You look keenly at him. You have
heard that he married a girl, a mere child, who had
herself no " say " in the matter. She was born at
Rome ; was young and good and beautiful. He
brought her to Arezzo, but with her came her reputed
parents, they who had sold her to a Title, and as they
believed, that they might better their own fortunes—
and hers (?)—

Before you allow your spirit to merge itself with that
of Guido, you, yourself cease to be Robert Browning,
and become " Half-Rome," finding for Guido " much
excuse ". . . . . Slowly, but truly, this feeling passes,
and you are swayed by its opposite. You become
" The Other Half-Rome," rather " siding with the
wife," who seems to you " a saint and martyr, both."
An interval, and you are neither this, nor that, . . .
but something bred of both. . . . You are neither more
nor less than the " Critical Mind," that dissertates
upon the " Case," free from feeling. You claim to
represent what the superior social section thinks, yet
wise and prudent in your own esteem you miss the

very soul of things and become the shuttlecock of
intellect. The game is wearisome ; you give it up.
You sink into a soft-cushioned chair, and so find yourself in the seat of Guido. You are in a small chamber,
adjoining the Court, not in the room where you first
started. Governor and Judge are there and you
speak. The voice is Guido's voice. You shift your
seat, your pallid cheek blanches, your tones become
more subdued, you are almost as " umble " as Uriah
Heap ; then mournful, satirical, fiery. . . . Yet
though now and again you " feel you have a fist,"
you eventually fold your arms, and make up your
mind, that you can do yourself best service by being
meek. How you look at your judges ! Your twitching
brow and wincing lip have been induced by the vigil-
torment. The day is over. You are tired, worn out,
and even the consideration of your fate that trembles
in the balance, cannot keep you longer awake, when,
the Court rises, and, for the time-being the trial is
over. The most terrific day is that which to-morrow
brings you. Reincarnated once again, you are this
time Guiseppe Caponsacchi, man and priest. Can
you comprehend the coil ? There you stand, suddenly
summoned from the exile into which you had, eight
months before been banished, into the presence of the
same Judges as those Guido had seen previously.
But strange, is it not, before you they keep silence.
You seem grown Judge yourself ! Your speech is
rapid, angry ; speech that smites blow on blow. It
may be that you have an *invisible* audience, as,
seeming-solitary man, you speak for God. 'Tis thus
you have your say and pass on.

On a low pallet, in the good house that helps the poor
to die, you have lain four days, a-dying. You are
so young, such a girl, scarce seventeen and a half
years old. You tell the story of your life—as if one
ever could really tell the story of one's life—you try
to explain the inexplicable to the common kindliness

about you. They have removed the little one, but a fortnight old, and soon, on the white bed, under the arched roof, they cover your face, but not before you've told whatever could be told . . . but the truth broke through your poor halting language and—escaped—. Not for want of the *will* to tell it, but simply because it was impossible to reduce it and confine it to words. Truth is ever elusive ! It becomes more elusive, as from the mind of Pompilia you pass successively into that of the two learned Advocates—Arcangeli and Bottini.—You make your " first speech for ' Guido ' 'gainst the Fisc " (Bottinius), or, being Bottinius you make the " last speech 'gainst Guido and his gang, with special end to prove Pompilia pure."

You leave the Court and make your way to the Vatican, and there, in a small room, little larger than a cell, you enter into the mind of Pope Innocent XII and with him go carefully and prayerfully over again the pros and the cons of the " crime."   In the room are a table and a chair, a crucifix, and an invisible legion of legions of thoughts. " Grave but not sad " you read the notes, and lay the papers down and muse, and take a turn about the room . . . open a huge volume, find the lines you seek, and bowing your head you confirm your final decision ; you write out three lines, pregnant with meaning and sign and seal the writing. You tinkle a bell and hand to the attendant the mandate to be carried to the Governor. Then, having made the momentous decision, you walk down the corridor, and, your conscience clear, partake of supper. . . . " The manner of the Judgment of the Pope." Once again you are Guido. Once again you must speak, for life is precious, and all the more so as you are in imminent danger of losing it. " Death's breath rivels up the lies," and the true words come at last. . . . You speak and despair, this last night of your life. . . . You are the same person as when you feigned humility, but you have now another voice. . . .

You are seated in no easy chair, as formerly, but, on a stone bench, in a close, fetid cell, " where the hot vapour of agony struck into drops on the cold wall runs down horrible worms, made out of sweat and tears." The whining has become screaming ; you rail with demoniac violence . . . and only at the last moment do you, Guido, call on your sainted wife . . . "*Pompilia will you let them murder me ?*"

It was thus that Robert Browning wrote his most wonderful story—" fancy with fact is just one fact the more." He wrote " I fused my *live* soul with that *inert* stuff," (the book of facts) and he asks "Lovers of *dead* truth, did ye fare the worse ? Lovers of *live* truth found ye false my tale ? "

BOOK No. II

"HALF-ROME"

BOOK No. II

My Dear Friend,

As " Half-Rome " thinks as I do I want to tell you what I think and so you shall have the equal opinion of " Half-Rome."

The crush about the Church is tremendous. It was the parish Church of the victims in days when they thought little of it. At one time they lived close by. You know the Church very well. Do you remember how small it is ? Maybe it has never looked smaller than when the lifeless two were laid out there ! Both the bodies were laid in the Church, two steps up, on the Chancel, just behind the little marble balustrade. They brought them up early in the morning. Pietro —I can only think of him with contempt—was laid to the right of the altar, and his wretched wife on the other side. Everybody who could press near enough was busy, counting stabs on her face. I wonder what she'd have thought of her own face if she could have seen it as I saw it ! *His* wounds were distributed all over his body. There's a silly story told, but some people profess to believe it, that Pietro's body turned round and rolled away from Violante's side, where it was first laid. If that's so, say I, why didn't it roll right down the Altar steps, through the nave and out of Church, and so deprive the whole of the curious multitude of the ugly object of their fascination ? If the corpse of the old man was as sensitive as all that, well, by getting away so, it would have paid back a few of the affronts this same Church had offered him by lending herself as a theatre for such acting as per-

13

haps few men have seen. Why 'tis common talk that at the same altar where he lies, to the same inch of step, was brought the babe for blessing after baptism, and there styled " Pompilia " and a string of names beside, by his bad wife, some seventeen years ago, when she had *purchased* the babe, simply to palm off on *him* as their own child ! What will not an old fool believe ? She had mercenary views too, for, if they could show a child they could also show the heir to property, which else must fail, with him.

Twelve years later, the wicked old fraud, Violante, brought the girl, a mere child, to the same Church and place, to link a new victim to the lie. She made this girl, her *reputed* daughter by Pietro, marry an honest man, and a man of birth, clandestinely, quite unbeknown to her silly old husband. She had to tell him later, but trust the cunning old thing to make good her case with that old fool ! That's four years ago ! The name of the man who was deceived into marriage with this Pompilia-girl was Guido Franceschini—Count—. Now mark me ! It was at this very spot in the Church, where these double deceptions took place, that the bodies were laid out and are now lying ! Doesn't this fact point to special design in Providence ?

You should have seen the multitude that flocked to the Church ! Rome was at the show. The people climbed up the columns, fought for spikes o' the chapel rail to perch themselves upon, jumped over and so broke woodwork, (painted like porphyry), the organ loft was crammed, and such was the crush that women were fainting, and little wonder ! Plenty of candles were set, a row all round, and one big taper at each head and foot. So people pushed their way and took their turn, saw, threw their eyes up, crossed themselves, gave place to pressure from behind, and since all the world knew the old pair, could talk the tragedy over from first to last. Even old Luca Cini, well over seventy years, was there. He stood leaning on his

staff, mute in the midst of the crowd, the whole man
one amaze. I spoke to him . . . he became reminis-
cent of " bodies set forth " which he had seen, when as
a tiny child he had stood holding his father's hand . . .
he was quite anticipatory of seeing the body of Pompilia, the young wife, laid out alongside the others . . .
I cut him short by telling him that the doctors gave her
longer . . . and asked him to give me an account of
the butchery. . . . He quite relished my request . . .
said " I like to teach a novice ; I shall stay," and he
did stay, and will !

His Eminence, the Cardinal, came by the private
door, to take his look. We were all hoping that young
Curate Carlo, who popped up when Cardinal arrived,
would give his account of the tragedy ; tell us, perhaps, how the wife's confession went. (Of course we
know that this morning she confessed her crime !)
Not he ! Nothing from him when the Cardinal was
there. He described the murder in a dozen words ;
turned it all back on the *Molinos,* the sect that teach
" philosophic love." But, we've heard all about
them, before. Well, never mind ! The whole murder's
maze is clear as daylight. . . . Do *you* believe that
Guido was so greatly to blame ? You do ? A cousin
of yours has told you so ? . . . Well now just listen
to me for a little ; I'll set you right. Here's the true
story from first to last.

The Comparini couple—Pietro and Violante—were
born in this quarter seventy years ago, of a middle-
class family, quite comfortably off . . . in fact their
means accumulated, as they'd no children, so that they
became wealthy—houses, land, and all that sort of
thing—He also had an interest in some property, which
interest, unless there were an heir, terminated with his
life. And so the trouble began. Its the old story,
ever new. He overlooked all the good he had, and
stared hard on Fortune's sole piece of forgetfulness—
the child that should have been and could not be.

Now Violante, though of grandmotherly age, one
day astonished her lord by telling him such " news "
as made the old fool agape. . . . She promised him,
in due time, an heir ! So, let it pass for the present,
Pompilia was born. The " father " went crazy with
joy ! When the babe was old enough he set aside all
other interests to amuse himself with her. Crawled
on all-fours, with his baby pick-a-back, romped, or
played at quiet games with her, and later set her up
against the wall and measured up her inches from top
to toe, to see what a great girl she had grown by twelve.
All this time he forgot to work, forgot even to look after
what he had, and certainly forgot to hoard, and lived
on what they had, until one day Poverty, going her
rounds, looked in at his door, and nodded, familiarly.
It was Violante who looked into the hag's face and pitted
her own wits to outwit the Jade. Pompilia of the
great eyes, and bountiful black hair, and early years,
should save them from the nip of hard-handed Poverty,
by a marriage of convenience. She should wed a
nobleman, rejoicing in a title, and with an old Palace
thrown in, and although not really wealthy, yet not
poor. So the marriage was rushed through, and once
again Pietro was kept in the dark. What matter that
Count Guido was old and ugly ? That in his household
was Guido's old lady mother, Beatrice, and his younger
brother ? Violante had her way, enticed the old nobleman into the marriage, and then left him to explain to
Pietro as best he could, and so at once placed him at a
disadvantage. He had to make his peace with the
girl's " father," and to transport the trio home to the
old Palace, which it was arranged should henceforth
be their home, and to propitiate his mother and younger
brother. Now, don't you think with me, that his back
was sufficiently burdened ? Just look at it and imagine
yourself Guido !—Do you ask what possessed him, and
do you tell me that he was not in his dotage ? Well,

what is Solomon's word on the subject of such fascinations ? " One black eye does it all."

Now comes the trouble. To the minds of Pietro and Violante had appeared such pictures of lordship and ladyship, and what life in a palace would be like ; such imaginings of feasting on rich foods, from plates of gold ; such wines and fruits, that when they found themselves in an old dilapidated stone palace, with only meagre fare, served on common plates of earthenware, and things in general far less comfortable than they had left, they began to shriek out their woes, and to cry out that they had been misled . . . duped, demanding to know where all the fine things that they had expected, were. " For *this*, have we exchanged our liberty, our competence, our darling of a child ? " they asked indignantly. " We are robbed, starved and frozen too ; we will have justice, justice if there be " was their cry. They spoke of the old lady-mother, as a dragon and a devil, though she was hard-taxed to feed all these extra mouths from her slender house-keeping purse, and Pietro went about trumpeting huge wrongs—in the market-place, at church, at Square's corner, streets' end, and the palace-steps, and refrained not to tell his tale on wine-house bench, and Violante did her best to spread the scandal. This went on for about four months, when they suddenly packed up and left, renouncing their share of the bargain—the payment of the greater part of the promised Pompilia-dowry—and left, for Rome. Now surely, you'll say, all the better for Guido. He had Pompilia with him, and now, perchance, a quiet life before him— with her. But you don't understand a woman of Violante's nature if that is what you think.

Just at this time the Pope attained eighty years and announced a Jubilee and a boon . . . short shrift and prompt pardon for light offences. Here was Violante's chance. She had a confession to make. Are you prepared to hear it ? Pompilia, as their

daughter, was a *fable, not* a *fact* ; Violante never bore a
child in her whole life ! If she could prove Pompilia
not her child then no child no dowry ! Guido's claim
to anything that they possessed was through his wife
as their daughter, and if her claim could be proved
baseless then his would of course be baseless too.
The biter bit, do you see ?

It mattered nothing to the hag, Violante, that she
made the sad tale of poor little Pompilia's birth and its
disgrace known to all Rome, and it was a horrible story,
a gutter tale that Violante told, of a wanton, who
professed to be a laundress, who eight months before
the birth of the babe had sold it to Violante. This ill-
conditioned creature, who found by chance, " Motherhood, like a Jewel in the muck," was a woman
" down in the deepest of social dregs."

Well might this story arouse the indignation of
Count Guido ! It was not the loss of the dowry ; it
was that Violante, by the tale, was affixing " the
brand of a bestial birth " on his young bride. Had he
been less a man he might have opened wide his door
and cast out his young wife, but not he ! Birth and
breeding and compassion too saved her such a scandal.
" She is young," he thought, " not privy to the treason,
punished most in the proclamation of it ; why make
her a party to the crime she suffered by ? " Then,
the black eyes were now her very own, not even
Violante's. Let her live, lose in a new air under a new
sun, the taint of the imputed parentage, truly or
falsely. Take no more the touch of Pietro and his
partner, anyhow ! All might go well yet.—So, at first,
she, herself, seems to have thought, for she wrote a
letter to Guido's brother, the Abate, who had effected
the match telling him how different the house was now
that the couple had gone ; " hell," she said, " was
heaven," and told how the house, which had lately
been distracted by their quarrels, was, now that they
had left, " quiet as Carmel where the lilies live." She

said, too, that though she, herself, had often found fault with little things, it was because Pietro and Violante had prompted her to do so. She alleged that they had bidden her follow them quickly ; fly from her husband's house, clandestinely ; pick up a fresh companion in her flight, and join them as soon as she could. But first she was to put poison in the posset cup, take all the money and jewels she could find, and then fire the house, and in the scurry and confusion that would follow, slip out, and off and away.

Meantime the Comparini couple had carried the matter to the Courts (at Rome) and the Abate had to stand forth and take his absent brother's part and defend *his* honour, as well as his own. The Court heard all and compromised, as it so often did. It would not take away the dowry now ; it would not play the game of " Pietro's child and now *not* Pietro's child." Then Pietro and his wife appealed ; this was followed by counter appeal by Guido, and so the action went on . . . tedious . . . heartbreaking.

But now all's clear for the young wife ; surely she'll walk warily and live quietly ? Not at all. Don't you think for a moment that once the doorpost has been marked by the enemy he'll keep away though you may stop up the door. . . . There's the window, and Pompilia heard his tap. Probably the " tap " was given with some of the hardened suggestions offered by Violante. She, the young wife started pitying herself as " too young and sprightly to be matched with a husband old beyond his age . . . found the house dull, and its inmates dead . . . so looked outside for life and light." And she did not look long, by the opportuneness of things, without seeing something that gladdened her eyes. " The man with the aureole, sympathy made flesh, the all-consoling Caponsacchi." A priest but every inch a man, for all that. The priest threw comfits into her lap, at the theatre, and was ever on the look out to express to her his sympathy and

admiration. Guido was busy with his accounts and
puzzling how to make little money do the most. He
was not at first suspicious, or jealous, or even fully
aware of things going on under his nose, but presently
the whispers became a buzz which he could not but hear,
and hearing heed.

> " I'll not have it
> I'll punish it
> I'll do this, that and the other,"

he declared, but O 'twas easy saying it ! At his first
hint of suspicion Pompilia made a mighty to do with
indignation and cried out to the Governor and the
Archbishop that she was wronged by such suspicion—
even sitting on the doorsteps and wringing her hands
in protest, and when the Archbishop came out to see
what it was all about flinging herself down at his feet
and shrieking out her wrongs ; eventually she fled
back to her husband's house.

Things got worse and worse between the ill-matched
two, until one April day, Guido awoke about noon,
to find that he had been drugged with opium, and that
his wife had fled, having taken with her money and
jewellery, after putting an opiate into the drink of
the whole household overnight—" this lamb-like innocent of fifteen years."

Caponsacchi had a friend . . . a cousin of Guido
. . . and he had assisted in working out the scheme.
After the house was ransacked the lady was led
downstairs and out of doors, guided and guarded
till, the city passed, "a carriage lay convenient
at the gate," into it she jumps, the priest after her,
" Whip, driver !—Money makes the mare to go, and
we've a bagful—take the Roman Road ! " This
they did and so obtained full eight hours start of Guido,
who directly he could shake off the effects of the drug
mounted horse and galloped after his runaway wife,
and the runaway priest. They were always ahead of
him until just in sight of Rome . . . the Osteria . . .

where was a post-house inn . . . there at the journey's
all but end . . . at daybreak Guido overtook them !
In the courtyard stood the priest, urging the drowsy
stable grooms to haste, harness the horses, have the
journey end, the trifling four-hours-running, so
reach Rome. Pompilia was still resting. In the
same room the two had spent six hours together . . .
and so were *lost thereby*.

Now, friend, I, as " Half-Rome " ask you what do
you think these two discovered ones did . . . how
comported they themselves in the immediate presence
of the angry, murderously angry, husband ? Think
you they both fell at his feet and implored for mercy,
and begged their lives ? Not they. Caponsacchi was
a true 'Paris' and Pompilia 'Helen.' " I interposed to
save your wife from death, yourself from shame, the
true and only shame : ask your own conscience else !
or, failing that what I have done I answer, anywhere.
Here, if you will ; you see I have a sword : or, since
I have a tonsure as you taunt, at Rome, by all means,—
priests to try a priest." So Guido called in the officers
of the law and they secured the priest, and then because
they would confound him, if they could, they took him
upstairs to where Pompilia slept, or feigned to sleep.
They burst into the bedroom and bade her rise. She
saw ; sprang upright ; sprang to her husband's side,
caught at the sword that hung there and in a moment
drew it out and flashed it in the face of Guido. The
sword of her lover had been taken from him and his
hands were held down. It was from no want of will
on Pompilia's part that she did not slay her husband,
the priest, and herself and so finish the tale just here,
but she fought her foes, one to six. They stopped
that but her tongue continued free and she told such a
tale of terrible sufferings endured at her husband's
hands that even the Guard pitied her, and execrated
the Count, and, " persecuting fiend " and " martyred
saint," were words passed between one and another.

They had appealed to Rome ; to Rome they were taken and Rome slightly punished the priest for imprudence by sending him to Civita ; and her they sent to a Sisterhood, a Penitentiary. Count Guido claimed in due form a divorce from his wife. This she met by a counter-claim for divorce on the grounds of his outrageous cruelty, and she mentioned as a part of it his mother's malice and his younger brother's hate. News came from the Sisterhood that Pompilia's health required more freedom than the irksome Convent walls permitted, and it was agreed that she should be sent to some sure friend's house and there kept inside. What house do you think she chose ? Why that of Pietro and Violante ! They took her into their house. *That* was poison sufficient for Guido, if you like ! In that Villa Pompilia gave birth to a child, said to be Guido's son and heir, or, if you will, Guido's heir but Caponsacchi's son.

Little wonder with all this that Guido's mind broke down and that " what was a brain became a blaze ! " When the Count first heard this thing he was at work on his farm among his vines. He instantly summoned his steward and called in the first four stout hearts and hard hands. . . . He'd had enough of law and law's delay ; he would go be himself the law. They all arrived at the Villa. He bade his servants stand aside. He could see the warmth and light within the doors. He knocked. " Who is it knocks ? " cried one.

" Guiseppe Caponsacchi ! " Guido replied.

> " And open flew the door : enough again !
> Vengeance, you know, burst like a mountain wave
> That holds a monster in it, over the house,
> And wiped its filthy four walls free again
> With a wash of hell-fire—father, mother, wife,
> Killed them all, bathed his name clean in their blood,
> And reeking so, was caught, his friends and he,
> Haled hither and imprisoned yesternight
> O' the day all this was."

Now the whole is known, and how the old couple
came to lie in state, though hacked to pieces . . .
while the wife . . . at day's end must die.

Now friend, I ask you what's the good of *law* in a
case of this kind ?

> " Call in law when a neighbour breaks your fence,
>   Cribs from your field, tampers with rent or lease,
>   Touches the purse or pocket,—but wooes your wife ?
>   No : take the old way trod when men were men."

So " Half-Rome " found *for Guido* much excuse.

BOOK No. III

" THE OTHER HALF-ROME "

BOOK No. III

"THE OTHER HALF-ROME"

My Dear Friend,
   Make no mistake ! I am not one to be taken in by
a fellow like Guido. I have seen his kind and style
before. He first appeared in Eden and hissed his
suggestion in the innocent's ear and he's been hissing
ever since in every ear that will lend itself and sometimes in those that won't. Why *I've* heard his hisses
time and again ! He, Guido, stabbed her, the poor little
Pompilia, for *failing* to do what, if he'd have been a man
he'd have stabbed her for *doing* ! I'm well aware what
" Half-Rome " is saying and how it says it ; but
give me half an hour of your time and I'll show the
other side of things ; I'll so show you that you'll
find the answer of Truth in your own heart. You may
very well assume that as a bachelor I know a great deal
about marriage. I know the rules of the " game "
and what is " *sport* " and what *isn't*. I've not practised Art, with a big A, for nothing ; I've not been all
an Eye, all an Ear, all Touch and Taste for nothing !
I've a clear vision in this affair, and I know Pompilia
to be as innocent as the proverbial heart of a child.
   She's still " living," she who never " lived " in its
best sense, the Pompilia denied by father and mother
and betrayed by her vile old husband ! I had a strange
feeling as I stood in that cell of a hospital-place, where
her poor face offered its wan smile. If I'd a wish to
sculpture a brow for Patience I'd use her's as my model.
A poor fragile flower-like body was hers. One of those
delicate things that bruise at the shadow of a blow . . .
but now pierced through and through with hate-holes

at the point of that cruellest of swords, a husband's.
Why her very soul, staying as it does among the body's
ruins, is testimony of the Virgin's pleasure in her. She
offered her poor little prayer, when first he struck her
that she might live long enough to confess and be
absolved. Her prayers have had little success in the
answers hitherto accorded by the listening Virgin, but
this time all too successful for still the child-wife,
child-mother lingers on. I should like to read a
book written by the blessed Virgin Mary herself on her
reasons for refusing or answering prayers ! I can almost
hear the Madonna say to Guido and all worldly men as
she looks at the pathetic face

> " There's anyhow a child
> Of seventeen years, whether a flower or weed,
> Ruined : who did it shall account to Christ—
> Having no pity on the harmless life
> And gentle face and girlish form he found,
> And thus flings back : go practise if you please
> With men and women : leave a child alone
> For Christ's particular love's sake ! "—

Why was this girl, this Pompilia dying here made
to have " undue experience of how much crime a heart
can hatch ? " I can only think it may be because
competitors, shall we say, for saintship are *spared*
nothing. It is not by sparing troubles and trials that
Saints are made. Better be a sinner if you'd be
immune from all such trials and tests.

It's a strange thing this life of ours. Consider
Pietro and Violante. Until seventeen years ago they
were happy enough. They were comfortably off ; none
envied them and none scorned. They had what they
needed and more of this world's trash, and they were
very well matched ; she was the man of the house and
he had the woman's nature. They had health and
peace of mind, until, one day the hiss entered in the
ear of Violante. It was when the interest, the income
was paid. Pietro sighed and Violante interpreted it.

Trust a woman's intuition for that. " Failing an heir,"
thought Pietro, " the money goes to strangers."
Violante let the sigh go past her for all that Pietro
knew for the time . . . but a few days later she told
her husband that there is no " too late " with God ;
that He had answered prayers though He'd tarried.
The years are naught to Him, she said, was not Sarah ?
—And then she told, coyly too, that to her was to
happen that great event of a woman's life, a child,
and to him that which should cause his old bones to
thrill with joy and happiness—fatherhood ! Now it
would be quite easy here to call him a stupid fool for
crediting such folly but would you doubt your *own* wife
if she came to you with such a tale and told in such a
way ? You'd find doubt harder so than faith, as Pietro
did. So then Pietro was gladdened, Violante satisfied
and who should care about an unknown inheritor to
defend him. As well take up a plea for the wind !
The child ? Well, what of *it* ? The child, an illicit
offspring, was bought, eight months before its birth,
of a wretched low-down mother . . . and so rescued
from disgrace and shame, and likely from a premature
death, as Violante thought. What then was the harm ?
She kept the truth back from old Pietro ; she kept,
or aimed to keep the money as she would, even after
death. " What so excessive harm is done ? " she
asked. To which demand the dreadful answer comes—
" For that same deed, now at Lorenzo's Church,

> " Both agents, conscious and inconscious, lie ;
> While she, the deed was done to benefit,
> Lies also, the most lamentable of things,
> Yonder where curious people count her breaths,
> Calculate how long yet the little life
> Unspilt may serve their turn nor spoil the show,
> Give them their story, then the Church its group."

Still, when all's said and done Pompilia's first twelve
or thirteen years were happy. To Pietro and to
Violante too, the childless couple, thus made parents,

those years were full of pleasant childish things. At times, even Violante, who in her secret heart knew other, almost believed the child was his and hers.

Its easy enough to picture the home life of these years ! The little one " grew in the midst of Pietro here and Violante there, each like a semi-circle with stret-ched arms, joining the other round her preciousness "— She grew tall and toward her twelfth year, womanly, and Pietro and Violante felt a nameless fear of so much and so quick growth. . . . One afternoon, when old Pietro dozed, and Pompilia worked away at her broider-frame three rooms from her " Mother," a smooth-mannered, soft-speeched, sleek-cheeked visitor, the notable Abate Paolo (Count Guido's younger brother—Guido Franceschini of Tuscany) called to speak with Violante.

You can see him, standing there, smoothing his great flap-hat, and his clerical stockings by turn, but all the time, as he speaks, keeping the thin clear grey hold of his eyes on her—He tells of the Tuscan House of Franceschini ; " very old," he says, " they are, but not rich as the vulgar would-be-rich think of riches ; and yet, not by any means poor." Then he introduces his brother's name, Guido, whose patron is one Cardinal Nerli. . . . Sighs and bemoans his brother's want of ambition . . . says that his brother, who is getting into years is home-sick, yearning for the old sights and old faces of Arezzo. Exclaims " Poor brother Guido ! All too plain he pines amid Rome's pomp and glare for dinginess and that dilapidated palace-shell ; . . . or for that absurd wild villa in the waste o' the hill side " . . . mentions the vines, and country life, and imparts the semi-secret information that nought else will serve Guido, " But that, to light his mother's visage up with second youth, hope, gaiety again, he must find straightway, woo and haply win and bear away triumphant back, some wife." Now the Abate is much troubled in case designing mothers should get

to hear of this intention and so introduce their daugh-
ters . . . and eventually shame the household with an
unfit wife for Guido. But, he says, he thinks he under-
stands his brother's heart and mind, better perhaps
than that brother does himself, and he adds, " We
want no name and fame, having our own : no worldly
aggrandisement—such we fly : but if some wonder of a
woman's heart were yet untainted on this grimy earth,
tender and true—tradition tells of such— . . . If
some good girl, . . . not wealthy . . . but with
whatever dowry came to hand, *there* were the lady-
love predestinate ! " This brings him to the crux of
the story ; and he informs Violante that he has heard
that there is in her house just such a pure lily-white
girl, a wife worth Guido's house and hand and heart !
He has spoken ; if Violante does not like the suggestion,
well then let her dismiss it . . . but . . . perhaps
she will think it over . . . and kissing Violante's
hand with a great air, he withdraws. Do you see
it all ?

Much astonished Violante then hastened to rouse up
sleepy Pietro and pour into his ears this mighty news.
He, good man, bethought him rather sadly of what the
loss of their darling would mean to them. But if it
were for her true good, why . . . he was not the man
to interpose. Yet he'd find out what folk said of the
Tuscan family. So, putting on his hat, he sallied out,
cane in hand, towards the fountain, where he knew
that idlers lounge. He here told his news. But
" the world," his world, standing agape and listening,
soon burst into laughter. " The Count Guido Franceschini is without money or means to support his Count-
ship . . . his cornfields are but stubble-fields, and his
palace a ruined brick-heap . . . sloth, pride, rapacity
were all that were left him. He had hung on to the
Cardinal's Court long enough, they said, as a parasite
and picker-up of crumbs . . . now he's tired of the trade
and wants to change town for country !

" ' Oh, make your girl a lady, an you list,
But have more mercy on our wit than vaunt
Your bargain . . . .
Why, Goodman Dullard, if a friend must speak,
Would the Count, think you, stoop to you and yours
Were there the value of one penny-piece
To rattle 'twixt his palms—or likelier laugh,
Bid your Pompilia help you black his shoe ? ' "
                So the gossips,

Home walked Pietro, to inform Violante of what had
been said to him, and to point out by way of comfort
that it was a solace in this trouble to have had the
opportunity of discovery so soon.

" The marriage thus impossible, the rest
Followed : our spokesman, Paolo, heard his fate,
Resignedly Count Guido bore the blow :
Violante wiped away the transient tear,
Renounced the playing Danae to gold dreams,
Praised much her Pietro's prompt sagaciousness,
Found neighbours' envy natural, lightly laughed
At gossips' malice, fairly wrapped herself
In her integrity three folds about,
And letting pass a little day or two,
Threw, even over that integrity,
Another wrappage, namely one thick veil
That hid her, matron-wise, from head to foot,
And, by the hand holding a girl veiled, too,
Stood, one dim end of a December day,
In Saint Lorenzo on the altar-step—
Just where she lies now and *that girl will lie*—
Only with fifty candles' company
Now—in the place of the poor winking one
Which saw,—doors shut and sacristan made sure,—
A priest—perhaps Abate Paolo—wed
Guido clandestinely, irrevocably
To his Pompilia aged thirteen years
And five months,—witness the Church register,—
Pompilia (thus become Count Guido's wife
Clandestinely, irrevocably his)."

Thus you see, my dear friend, how very little the
innocent lamb had to do with this bargain which so
concerned her !

When the " transfer was complete," then the cunning
Violante told Pietro what she had done and with tears
and excuses she, eventually, pacified his wrath.

By the mere marriage Guido gained a dowry, by
right of his wife, Pompilia, for the parents cast their
lot into the lap of the daughter and so Guido took by
right

> " Pietro's whole having and holding, house and field,
> Goods, chattels and effects, his worldly worth,
> Present and in perspective, all renounced,"

in his favour. Even the principal would later come to
him, should Pietro and Violante predecease him. He
on his part was to house and board the couple, who
would accompany their darling child,—fromw hom they
could not bear to be separated,—to Arezzo.

But now what a change came over Guido ! Never
had the two, Pietro and his wife, known such a four
months ! They had experience in the tumble-down
old Palace at Arezzo, with Count Guido's domineering
old mother and his insolent younger brother and the
Count himself, of

> " how craft and greed,
> Quickened by penury and pretentious hate
> Of plain truth, brutify and bestialise,—
> Four months' taste of apportioned insolence,
> Cruelty graduated, dose by dose
> Of ruffianism dealt out at bed and board."

Such were the miseries and abuses that the Comparini
had to suffer in victuals and in harsh treatment that
they were obliged to return to Rome after a few months;
for Pietro was locked out of the house and had to go to
the tavern to lodge ; and these abuses were *for the
purpose* of *shortening their lives*, either *by their sufferings*
or *the fury caused thereby*. The fraudulent pretentions
of the Franceschini are obviously proved by the rent-
rolls taken from the public records of the city of
Arezzo. From these it is shown that Guido did not

D

possess *any* of the settled property mentioned in the
note.   It is *also* untrue that he and his family enjoyed
the highest rank of nobility in the city, because, from
other extracts drawn from the public records of the
city, it is quite evident that his family is only of
secondary rank.

Now, Violante, smarting under the abuses and
injuries received in the house of the Franceschini,
and feeling remorse of conscience, and believing that
these troubles may have been signs of the displeasure of
God at her former deception connected with the child's
birth, and constrained by her Confessor at the time of
Jubilee to reveal to her husband that Francesca Pompilia was not their daughter, but of false birth, on this
occasion disbosomed all to him ! Had he been told of
this trick but six months before, he would have felt
it very differently, but now at the entry of this news,
he leapt for joy, metaphorically speaking, for by a
knowledge of this fact he could strike a deadly blow at
the pride of the Franceschini in the revelation that
Pompilia, whom he had married, was of ignominious
parentage ! It was in the spring of 1694 that Pietro
brought suite before Judge Tomati for the recovery of
the dowry moneys paid to Franceschini—a bitter
humiliation to the greedy poverty of the family of
Count Guido.

He, speaking through his brother, Abate Paolo,
pronounced the story one long lie " lied to blot him
though it brand themselves."

The Court resorted, as the Oracle of old, to ambiguous
compromise.   Its decision was very strange.   It
actually decided that Pompilia was *a changeling* . . .
but willed that the dowry, though not hers at all,
should yet be his, if not by right then grace !—Part
payment for the plain injustice done ! It also said
that Pietro's own estate, apart from the dowry,
must be given back to him, he having been no party
to the cheat.

Immediately both sides appealed : Pietro asked " Do you say that Pompilia is *not* my child ? Why give her my child's dowry ? "

Guido said " Have I a right to the dowry, then why not to the rest as well ? "

Then answered the law " *Reinvestigate the case.*" And so the matter is still hung up ! Guido, after the Court's decision, and while his appeal against its judgment was unheard, was filled with an immense hate and the only creature on which he could expend it was his poor girl-wife. Interest demanded that he should keep her while the question of the dowry still held, but hatred moved him so intensely that he took the course of carefully torturing her, hoping, in his fiendish heart, to cause her to take, as though spontaneously, " the road of shame."—If he goaded her sufficiently would she not break out in full revolt, and run away and " so should the loathed form and detested face launch themselves into hell and there be lost while he looked over the brink with folded arms." He deliberately thought out the whole scheme. He drafted a letter in pencil, to his brother, the Abate, and made Pompilia trace · it over in ink (she couldn't write) and sent it, pretending it was her letter. It was a vile letter, full of lies, stating that Pietro and Violante before they fled had revealed to her their malice, bidding her poison all the inmates of the household, find a paramour, and then, burning down the house, to flee to Rome. The letter despatched he started to plague Pompilia. He gave her streams of insults, and did not spare her from blows, and more than once he provided himself with a sword and fire-arms to take her life. She was always shut up in her room, and her fears were greatly increased, because she saw her husband mix a poison, with which he threatened that he would take her life without the uproar attendant on the use of arms, and he told her that none would know of it or how she died, and that *he* would go unpunished !

She was only sixteen, a mere girl, but an ancient in suffering. He did all this to take vengeance upon her *for his own trick,* by which he had been deluded !

Twice she escaped and appealed on the first occasion to Monsignor, the Bishop, and on the second occasion to the Governor of the City. But it was almost like a nightmare : the frightened child found that these men were old friends of her husband's family ! They seem to have remonstrated mildly with Guido, but of course did " not mean to suggest that he should not be master in his own house "—Then she appealed to a simple friar of the City and told him how she was so *utterly miserable* and terrified that she contemplated suicide and begged him for pity's sake to write plain, for one who could not write, a little prayer to Pietro and Violante, that, even if they were not her parents they should for love's sweet self attempt to save her. At first the friar promised to do this for her, then, thinking over his promise, at night, he felt that he might get himself into serious trouble if he wrote, and, so " sighing at matrimony as a profound mistake," he gave the business up. Once more poor Pompilia, in an agony of mind, intrusted herself to Canon Conti, telling *him* of her miseries and perils and her just fears. He was a near relative of the Franceschini, but he was touched by a living compassion, and was moved to free her, by pity, from the grievous state in which she was. He knew that there was only one hope for her, one chance, and that was by flight from her husband's house. He could not aid her himself, but he suggested that there was no better person for the purpose than Canon Giuseppe Caponsacchi, his friend and intimate, " whose spirit had stood every test."

So it came about, was brought about by the Powers that be, that

> " On a certain April evening, late
> I' the month, this girl of sixteen, bride and wife

Three years and over,—she who hitherto
Had never taken twenty steps in Rome
Beyond the church, pinned to her mother's gown,
Nor, in Arezzo, knew her way through street
Except what led to the Archbishop's door,—
Such an one rose up in the dark, laid hand
On what came first, clothes and a trinket or two,
Belongings of her own in the old day,—
Stole from the side o' the sleeping spouse—who knows ?
Sleeping perhaps, silent for certain,—slid
Ghost-like from great dark room to great dark room,
In through the tapestries and out again
And onward, unembarassed as a fate,
Descended staircase, gained last door of all,
Sent it wide open at first push of palm,
And there stood, first time, last time and only time,
At liberty, alone in the open street,—
Unquestioned, unmolested, found herself
At the city gate, by Caponsacchi's side,
Hope there, joy there, life and all good again
The carriage there, the convoy there, light there
Broadening into a full blaze at Rome
And breaking small what long miles lay between ;
Up she sprang, in he followed, they were safe,"

The journey was a headlong flight. There was not a moment lost, except for changing horses, and the compassionate Caponsacchi, on their arrival at Castelnuovo, listened to the words of the troubled, tired overwrought and prostrate girl, as she told him that "though Count Guido were but a furlong off, just on me, I *must* stop and rest awhile ! " A word by the Canon to the host at the tavern where they were to get new horses, and the weary and worn Pompilia was shown to a bed, where she laid down her tired, wellnigh exhausted body and slept profoundly. Caponsacchi in the room below, and about the yard, now in, now out, eagerly awaited the arrival of fresh horses to continue the journey to its end.

But, O tragedy of grief and disappointment, the poor little sleeper was awakened by the rude harsh voices of men, in her sleeping apartment, and the first face she saw, as the light streamed on it, was the angry, ugly, murderous face of her cruel tormentor, Guido. Her would-be deliverer, Caponsacchi, was helpless, held a prisoner in the hands of the officers of the law who had been summoned by Guido's instructions. " Then," says Pompilia, " Not for my sake, but for his who had helped me—I sprang up, reached him (Guido) with one bound, and seized the sword of the felon, trembling at his side, unsheathed the thing and would have pinned him to the wall with it, and left him there . . . but men interposed—disarmed me and gave his life to him again." Now, friend, I ask you did that sound like the voice of a frightened, guilty woman, who had wronged her husband and disregarded her own purity and modesty ? She said more, all on fire as she was, at the tender age of sixteen years, she rebuked her vile husband for the tricks and abuses which he had employed, and for the threats and blows he had so often given her, and for the poisonous drugs that he had prepared to take her life, and she declared to those around her that she had been obliged to do as she had done, to find an escape by flight from graver peril, and to return to the parental love of the Comparini, who had raised her as their daughter ; and that she had always been careful to keep her wifely honour intact.

Alert, calm, resolute and formidable stood Caponsacchi as he first met Guido, before ascending to the room where Pompilia rested. He said, calmly, to the angry husband, " I have saved your wife from death ; there was no other way but this ; Of what do I defraud you except death ? Charge any wrong beyond, I answer it " . . . " If as a man, then much more as a priest I hold me bound to help weak innocence : if so my worldly reputation burst, being the bubble it is, why, burst it may : blame I can bear though not blameworthiness. . . . Enough that first to last I never touched her lip nor she my hand, nor either of us thought a thought, much less spoke a word which the Virgin might not hear. Be *that* your question, *thus* I answer it," was his further speech before the Court, which sentenced him to three years relegation to Civita and her to detention in a Convent. That was all the answer the law gave Guido, clamoured he never so loudly his wife should be declared an adulteress and that to him should pass all the gain of the dowry. Thus, this avaricious old hypocrite did all this for the sole object of gain, that is to win the dowry.

Five months later, " the Convent's self made application bland, that, since Pompilia's health is fast o' the wane, she may have leave to go combine her cure of soul with cure of body, mend her mind together with her thin arms and sunk eyes that want fresh air, say outside the Convent-wall,"—and so it came about that " Francesca Pompilia, wife of Guido Franceschini of Arezzo, was placed ' at liberty,' . . . and promised to keep to this home of Pietro, situated in Via Paulina, as a safe and secure *prison*, and not to leave it either by day or by night, nor to show herself at the door or open windows, under any pretext whatsoever, etc., with the thought of having to return again to prison." Into this bond, under a penalty of 500 scudi, Pompilia entered with the Apostolic Chamber.

Two months later *Guido* was notified by his brother, the Abate, that " by happy providence a son and heir was born to him, Guido, in the Villa." He added " I shall have quitted Rome, ere you arrive, to take the one step left." Pompilia named her boy " Gaetano," after the saint to whom she made her vows. And Guido ? Here now he saw, if ever—his chance ! He would kill her whom he had vowed to " husband " —his 16 year old wife—and her parents, and then " only a child would remain, depositary of all, that Guido might enjoy his own again."—So with his heart given over to hatred and greed " He rushed to Vittiano, found

four sons o' the soil, brutes of his breeding," and after
he had harangued them and told them what he desired
of them, they all took horse, plied spur and so arrived,
all five of them, at Rome, on Christmas Eve. Guido
stopped at Ponte Milvio, where there was a villa of his
brother's.   There he remained in. hiding, with his
followers, until a time opportune for the execution of
his designs should come.   They spied out all the ways
of the Comparini family and on January 2nd, which was
Thursday, at about seven o'clock in the evening, " the
dreadful five felt fingerwise their way across the town
by blind cut and black turns

> " To the little lone suburban villa ; knocked—
> ' Who may be outside ? ' called a well-known voice.
> ' A friend of Caponsacchi's bringing, friends,
> ' A letter.'
> ' Come in ' bade poor Violante, cheerfully,
> Drawing the door-bolt : *that* death was the first,
> Stabbed through and through.   Pietro, close on her heels,
> Set up a cry—' Let me confess myself !
> ' Grant but confession.   Cold steel was the grant.
> Then came Pompilia's turn."

She, poor child, in this crisis extinguished the light,
hoping thus to escape the assassins, and ran to the
neighbouring door of a locksmith crying out for help.
But when she saw that Guido was provided with a
lantern she went to hide under the bed ; she was
dragged out and barbarously attacked, twenty-two
wounds being dealt her.

Then, leaving her for dead, with the two others, they
escaped, . . . They had forgotten just the one thing
more which saves i' the circumstance, the *ticket* which
puts post horses at a traveller's use :

> " So all on foot, desperate through the dark
> Reeled they like drunkards along open road,
> Accomplished a prodigious twenty miles
> Homeward, and gained Baccano very near,

Stumbled at last, deaf, dumb, blind through the feat,
Into a grange and, one dead heap, slept there,
Till the pursuers hard upon their trace
Reached them and took them, red from head to heel,
And brought them to the prison where they lie.
The couple were laid i' the Church two days ago,
And the wife lives yet by miracle."

Now friend, what think you of Guido ?

BOOK No. IV

" TERTIUM QUID "

BOOK No. IV

"TERTIUM QUID"

My Dear Friend,

By the by what is " a friend " ?

What a satisfying thought it is to me that I'm not
of the dolts and fools, and that you are not of the fools
and dolts of this mad city, and that we can stop our
ears and shut out the rabble brabble of those who are !
They are a deal worse than silly children ;—needs must
see the whole play ; have the puppets actually *before*
them ; not a man Jack or a woman Jill, can see as far
as to the end of his or her own nose. So, forsooth
they must have a so-called Trial, *to manifest* Truth.
As if the " Trial " had not been proceeding in the face
of us all for the last three years! Why you and I, and
say another of our Class, and intelligence, could settle
the entire matter with a word or a wink, whereas, look
you, they will have a leash of lawyers, two on each side,
and spend a mint of money—bah—

What's that, you say ?—You ask if she's dead. No,
she's *not* dead but as good as " stretched symmetrical
beside the other two " ; just so I may say that though
he's not judged yet he's as *good* as judged, so do the
facts abound and superabound. Let us lift the case
into the light of intelligence, shall we ?—Now first I
should like you to appraise this fact : the episode is one
in burgess-life ; it is a pleb episode, and everything
connected with it. Why bless me people talk as though
they had to do with the élite, instead of the plebs !
Listen, and look, my august friend. This Pietro, this
Violante, lived their life at Rome in the usual selfish
pleb way of those who are comfortably off. The com-

mendations of their neighbours gladdened them. " No wine like Pietro's," or neighbourly sighs from heads turned to look at " the load of lace that came to pray " in Violante. This kind of indulgence ended, at fifty, in the fashion that it usually does,—even in our class— in debt—then the buzz of creditors begins ; One of them starts it by asking " If Pietro drop out who pays ?" None being able to point to a surety, they come up in a body to Pietro and clamour to be paid.

What does he do ? O ! he qualifies for a " pauper- saint "—one of the Pope's tame ravens, his holiness playing Providence. Just what the mob admires ! Of course, it's our set that's really taxed to pay for such selfish, worthless human slugs as they.

Violante doesn't quite like receiving this papal charity ; it hurts her pride ; neighbours *will* talk and remember,—besides there's no wine now, for a friend to take, and her own lace looks so frittered . . . she suddenly makes up her mind, sees the thing to do, and with a prayerbook under her arm posts off apparently to Church, but actually to a " poor child of Eve," nominally a washerwoman. Violante's business with her was a bargain, which " the laundress " concludes thus :—

> " Then, six months hence, that person whom you trust,
> Comes, fetches whatsoever babe it be ;
> I keep the price and secret, you the babe,
> Paying beside for mass to make all straight :
> Meantime, I pouch the earnest-money piece."

The flushed Violante gropes her way down the stairs, to the street, and gains the Church in time for the *Magnifi- cat.* You of course remember the words " My reproof is taken away and blessed shall mankind proclaim me now,"—Then back to her husband to tell him how at last "orisons and works of charity " have borne fruit in the autumn of his life, . . . and the result is like to be an heir.

Well, what follows ? In due time he finds himself the
sire indeed of this Francesca Vittoria Pompilia and the
rest of the names whereby he seals her his, next day.
Don't you call this a complete crime ? Lies to God and
man, robbery of the proper heirs thus foiled o' the due
succession and robbery of God through the Confessor's
ear !

You know Violante's capability of crime now. Not
that she allowed herself to think of it as a black,
hard, cold crime ! She soon decked it out prettily as
nature decks a hard stone kicked up in the middle of a
field. Do you want to see the grasses and mosses or wild
flowers she dressed it with ? There was the Joy
of the husband, the saving of a precious child,—a kind
of rose above the dungheap—Why, moralist, the sin
has saved a soul ! Look further. You would not,
would you, deny that the proper process of unsinning
sin is to begin well-doing somehow else ? Well this
" gift of God," this child flung into Pietro's lap steadied
him in a moment, set him straight on the good path he'd
been straying from, . . . self-denial became easy for
the child's sake. Debts were paid, habits reformed,
expense curtailed, and the dowry set to grow. But if
Pietro reformed—who had not sinned in the matter—
what think you of Violante ? She became a text for the
district : —

> " Oh, make us happy and you make us good !
> It all comes of God giving her a child :
> Such graces follow God's best earthly gifts ! "

Time passed ; the child grew ; the " parents " saved ;
the savings should make a common heap, and go
with the dowry, to be followed presently by the
heritage that would be hers . . . a " thumping purse "
should be this young beauty's.

There was an empty purse whose owner was
looking eagerly about to fill it. It belonged to Guido,

Count Guido Franceschini, the head of an old family in Arezzo, old to that degree they could afford to be poor better than most, the case is common too. This Count Guido had a brother, Abate Paolo, who served a patron-Cardinal, Nerli. An astute minded man was Paolo . . . he looked at the cards in his brother's hand . . . and helped him to handle them. Together they went to see and chat . . . with a woman-dealer in perukes, whom the Abate had helped to settle in the shop she then kept. *She* of course, the Abate's gossip, was familiar with the names of those eligible for marriage and possessed of means. The Abate promised this woman a present when a wedding should take place between Count Guido, his brother, and anyone named by her. And she plumped out Pompilia's name the first. Told of the household's way ; of easy Pietro and shrewder Violante and praised the black hair and large eyes of the tall innocent maiden.

The Abate went to wait on Madam Violante, sending his brother meantime to wait about in the Cardinal's ante room. Cardinals are not averse to a lord or so among the loungers. Abate Paolo had not much trouble in convincing Violante. Her practical answer was, " Yours be Pompilia, hers and ours that key to all the glories of the greater life ! There's Pietro to convince ; leave that to me ! "

The bargain amounted to this : —

> " I Guido truck my name and rank
>   For so much money and youth and female charms."—
> " We Pietro and Violante give our child
>   And wealth to you for a rise 'i the world thereby."

Now that sort of truth as long as it's kept in the brain shocks none, but if it is to be spoken it must be put into a lie, which must serve as decent wrappage. " According to the *words* each cheated each, but in the inexpressive barter of thoughts, each did give and did take the thing designed, the rank on this side and the

cash on that." . . . But, as it chanced, one party had
the advantage, *saw* the cheat of the other first, and
kept its own concealed. And the luck of the first
discovery fell, beside, to the least adroit and self-
possessed o' the pair. 'Twas foolish Pietro and his
wife saw first—the nobleman was penniless,—and
screamed ' We are cheated.' "

Guido's answer was so effective that long before five
months were out they—the old couple—were asking
from what was once their wealth just so much as would
help them back to Rome. Now can you wonder that
robbed, as they felt they were of child and means,
Violante's conscience began to prick . . . and pricked
her so effectually that she cried out her tale of the
substitution of the child ? Opportune, was it ? Well,
Violante's conscience was doubtless well adjusted to
keep time. See, had it become active sooner, Pietro
might have resented such activity, but now, just now,
why seems almost like revenge . . . if *not* our child
then she carries no dowry ! So Pietro the easier forgave
his erring wife ! Hear Guido's answer :—" My being
poor was a mere bye-circumstance. I gave my name
and title as promised ; you supplied your daughter
and your ducats ; now you would contest my right to
either ducats or daughter ; nay more ; would insist
and persist in dragging my name into the slush and
mud and filth of what ? No, no ; Your lie is too
enormously obvious . . . it is hatched of malice. I'll
answer it by revenge, strong and bitter as I can
make it."

Now, I ask you, friend and, with me, observer of men,
women and things, which of the two here sinned the
most ? Which brownness is least black ? This is the
glow of his thought : " Plague her—Pompilia,—I
plague *them* threefold . . . but how plague her with
impunity to myself ? . . . Why . . . drive *herself* to
plague herself—Herself disgrace herself and so disgrace

E

them who would disgrace me "—Ay Guido ! Dost see,
friend ? And so did

> " rage and hate so work in him,
> Their conduct proved the horrible conceit
> That he should plot and plan and bring to pass
> His wife might, of her own free will and deed,
> Relieve him of her presence, get her gone,
> And yet leave *all the dowry safe behind* "—

Guido, not being clown but nobleman, practised the
finer vengeance. 'Twas consistent so. See him at
work then, pencilling out the letter which he is later
to guide Pompilia's hand to trace in ink. So, she who
could neither read nor write, was made to declare to
her brother-in-law, the priest, how her " parents "
had bidden her " follow them, poison her husband,
rob the house, set fire to it and fascinate a brave youth
to bring her on to Rome, to their home."—Pompilia
knew nothing of the contents of the letter ; she
obediently traced the characters, Guido's hand over
hers, and there her part ended. Nor when the letter
was completed was the pressure on the poor child
lessened . . . rather increased. " All sort of torture
was piled, pain on pain, . . . month by month, week by
week, day by day and hour by hour . . . . Close,
closer and yet closer still with pain." And why ?
To force her to the only outlet from the encroaching
pain. . . . Whereat stood Caponsacchi, who, as it
seemed to her, cried, " This way, out by me !
Hesitate one moment more and the fire shuts out me
and shuts in you ! Here my hand holds you life out ! "
What would *you* have done friend ?

  Now this is, of course, Pompilia's tale ! One better
than Eve goes our Pompilia. Eve : " The serpent
tempted me and I did eat." Pompilia : " Adam so
starved me I was fain accept the apple any serpent
pushed my way." *But Guido has his version* of things.
He cites as a witness a serving-wench who declares that
she carried letters between the two. Caponsacchi

admits that he received letters, and was revolted by them, and answered them. Pompilia admits that she received letters from the priest, but not knowing how to read, burnt them. She objects that she couldn't write. Caponsacchi says that out of deep pity for the sufferings of the young wife he decided to help her escape from her husband.

The next stage of the story—play, if you will,— shows Guido in pursuit, coming up with the fugitives at the inn, and causing both to be arrested then and there and sent to Rome for judgment on the case— and thither, with all his armoury of proofs betook himself. His blunder was that as an outraged husband he appealed to law. Why, he should have cleared things on the spot, by slaying, or endeavouring to slay, his foe, the lover of his wife, as he professed he believed the priest to be. One had recognised in that the power of the pulse, but when he appeals to law " offers the hole in his heart, all fresh and warm for scrivener's pen to poke and play about "—Oh, let him not plead irrepressible just wrath and rage. Such rage is a convenient afterthought, and neither more nor less ! See him sneaking in at Court door and Church porch with " I have lost my honour and my wife, and being moreover an ignoble hound, I dare not jeopardise my life for them ! "

See Religion and Law lean forward from their chairs, with a " Well done good and faithful servant ! " Ay, they not only applaud him but would punish him should he do otherwise !

Priest, wife and husband each tells the story with the result that the Courts neither condemn nor acquit. The wife is sent to a House of the Convertites ; the priest is relegated to Civita, out of harm's way ; the husband is ordered to refund the money he had received from Pietro, *except the dowry*. The brother Abate bustles about and does his best, and he's kept busy, for his brother has three suits pending in the Courts.

At such a crisis happened to Guido the strangest accident of all—the wife's withdrawal from the Convertities, visit to the Villa where her parents lived, and the birth there, of *his babe*.   What is all this but a thunderclap of surprise ?

Then Guido *acts* ;   his brother Paolo vanishing, being swept off somewhere ! maybe moved out of the way for the purpose.   Guido comes to terms with four peasants, young and bold, and starts for Rome the Holy ; reaches her at very holiest, for 'tis Christmas Eve ; they hide a week but they contrive in that time to observe a great deal.   They *complete* their *plan*.

> " The five proceed in a body, reach the place.
> —Pietro's, by the Paolina, silent, lone,
> And stupefied by the propitious snow,—
> At one in the evening : knock : a voice
> ' Who's there ? '
> ' Friends with a letter from the priest your friend,'
> At the door straight smiles old Violante's self.
> She falls,—her son-in-law stabs through and through,
> Reaches thro' her at Pietro—' With your son
> This is the way to settle suits, good Sire ! '
> He bellows ' Mercy for heaven, not for earth !
> Leave to confess and save my sinful soul,
> Then do your pleasure on the body of me ! '
> —' Nay father, soul with body must take its chance ! '
> He presently got his portion and lay still.
> And last Pompilia rushes here and there
> Like a dove among lightnings in her brake,
> Falls also : Guido's this last husband's act.
> He lifts her by the long dishevelled hair,
> Holds her away at arms' length with one hand
> While the other tries if life come from the mouth—
> Looks out his whole heart's hate on the shut eyes,
> Draws a deep satisfied breath, ' So—dead at last ! '
> Throws down the burden on dead Pietro's knees,
> And ends all with ' Let us away, my boys ! ' "

> " And as they left by one door, in at the other
> Tumbled the neighbours—for the shrieks had pierced
> To the mill and the grange, this cottage and that shed.
> Soon followed the Public Force ; pursuit began

Though Guido had the start and chose the road.
So, that same night was he, with the other four,
Overtaken near Baccano,—where they sank
By the wayside, in some shelter meant for beasts."

As they are brought back to Rome, Guido, unable to
understand how anyone could have informed against
him, asks how they found out that it was he who did the
deed. " Who told you pray ? "
" Why, naturally, your wife ! "
Down Guido drops o' the horse he rode,—they have
to steady and stay at either side the brute that bore
him, bound, So strange it seemed his wife should live
and speak ! (She was not dead when I arrived just
now.)
It is said that she prayed to the Virgin that she
might live long enough to tell the truth, to make the
truth apparent for God's sake, lest men should believe
a lie.—Friend, an old question, What is Truth ? But
I can show you another reason why she'd tell " the
truth." By doing so she'd take a last revenge ; drag
down the hated Guido with her to the dark, and
set her lover free ; for he, though still at Civita, is
imperilled sore by the new turn things have
taken. They've sent for him and, who knows, he
may be punished still. Yet see how she strengthens
the case for him, by showing up Guido's villainy !
Undoubtedly no pains ought to be spared to give the
mob an inkling of our lights ! *Each* party wants too
much, claims sympathy for its object of compassion
more than *just*. Cry the wife's friends, " O the enormous crime caused by no provocation in the world ! "
Why here you have the awfulest of crimes, for
nothing ! Hell broke lose on a butterfly ! A dragon
born of rose-dew and the moon ! *Yet* if we look at the
monster Guido, we see mere man—born, bred and
brought up in the usual way. His mother loves him,
still his brothers stick to the good fellow of the boyish
games and all kinds of people, including Church

dignatories are willing to speak of his past and vouch for his future !

Perhaps good friend, wise friend, *you'll* give judgment in this case—

What ! You prefer to go to the pictures and see a Yankee woman electrocuted and saved by an ingenious American wireless trick ?

Well, I hope 'tis not for nothing I've written you . . . You know at least as much about it as all London . . . and Oxford ?

BOOK No. V

"COUNT GUIDO FRANCESCHINI"

BOOK No. V

"COUNT GUIDO FRANCESCHINI"

MY DEAR FRIEND,

I have lived this week as Guido. You, who know so well how little I can stand physical torture will no doubt be surprised to learn that the " vigil-torment " turned out to be no torment at all, but that blessed aid, a counter-irritation. I took the reverend Court by surprise, much as, no doubt, I shall take you by this record. They offered me " Velletri "—I couldn't help the ironical " There ! why, 'tis wine, Velletri,—and not *vinegar and gall,* So changed and good the times grow ! " I took but a sip . . . clear-mindedness is essential to me just now, for I'd save this head, if it's only for the old lady mother's sake ! Sitting in the fire-glow she'll think it back to baby-days, when in her lap it rested. Its scarcely rested since !

It was a study that even the racking could not put me off, to watch the faces of the Court as they watched mine. Faith, but I'm hard to read ! The mask I wear has taken thirty years amid the reverends this and that to fashion, and truth, I'm so accustomed to it that at times I doubt which is the real face, the face of me.—But friend, you who have looked beneath this mask of me, and seen another Guido than the world sees, let me just sketch briefly and crudely, the life-lines that I drew for them to scan.—I scorned to beat about the bush . . . I told them that their application of the rack to force from me the truth was pains taken to make a stone roll down the hill ! The Court sat as though carved, or turned by spell to stone as I said slowly in measured tones,

" I killed Pompilia *Franceschini*, Sirs " (Friend
mark my name attached to what was mine). " Killed,
too the Comparini."

There's the irregular deed : but what's a deed, an
Act, and that act hardly to be packed with all the
thoughts and fancies that went to its making. Its the
interpretation that's everything, as every churchman
holds from the most reverend his holiness to the humble
prisoner before you, who's here because of his very
fidelity to the Church. That moved them! You should
have seen the Court twisting itself into one note of
interrogation. A smile, half incredulous, diffused
itself into atmosphere, and I started sketching, sketching out and filling in that picture that I would should
save my head. First my stroke showed the long line
of the noble Arezzo family—the family-tree—tracing
it down to this twig, this dried twig, myself. Weeds,
that crept about the foot of the old tree, I showed,
had since sprung up, and even shut out light and sunshine from its boughs—and offered shade and shelter to
the very insects that sucked away its sap. Then I
cleaned the figure from the board and sketched again,
and this time showed them the life of Guido, me, their
prisoner now ; their faithful servitor for thirty years,
until that one sad, mad day, when tired, and sick of
waiting for the favours to come, I turned my face away
from all the mouldy promises of time and looked home-
wards, towards Arezzo, toward the lonely mother
getting old and with never a grandchild of her name to
gladden her—she having given my two younger
brothers to the Church,—and as I say, I thought of her,
my lady-mother, and of my father and his father and
the whole line of them, back and back and ever back,
not a commoner among them—all noblemen :—and of
my mother's grief lest the ancient line should die out
—in Church promises,—I was tired . . . disappointed
. . . I would leave Rome and go back to Arezzo, and
get the country air, and time the thrushes, and bring

a smile on the face of the waiting mother. It was in this mood that brother Paolo caught me and whispered the apt word—a wife, with just the proper dowry sufficient.—He said more ; " Leave it to me good brother," and before the week was gone his brotherly solicitude had found " it " in Pietro and Violante and their daughter. " She's young, pretty and rich : you are noble, classic, choice," he said. Then asked " Is it to be a match ? " " A match," said I. Done ! He proposed all, I accepted all. And we performed all. So I said and did simply. That was plain and clear enough for them, wasn't it ? I felt their question. " You mean to stand there and avow all this, without shame, that you dared *buy* a girl, of an age that your own grandchild might have been, buy her, this child, as you might ox or ass. Are flesh and blood a ware ? Are heart and soul a chattel ? " I had my answer then. Where was the wrong, I argued ; had I not to give of equal value ? What is the meaning of *Society* if *honour of birth*, such as that of the Franceschini, has no value ? Why Society goes to the ground. Its rules are idiots' ramblings. Admit, as you must my lords, that honour is a privilege, and the question follows, what is it worth ?

So then it was my rank, and I'd some small property too, against, what ? their no-rank, some wealth and some youth on the part of the daughter. I thought that a square deal ! What if it had been, say, the niece of one of your lordships there ? And those my offer most concerned, Pietro and Violante, did they cry out ? Not they ; they acceded promptly. It was only after the bargain was struck they repented them, no doubt, but so did I. . . . That after-thought is incident to all the folk who buy ! Among other charges brought against me is that I made myself out to be richer than I proved. And if I did, what does that matter . . . it was a sop to the world, *our* world ; it did not, could not affect the essence of the bargain which was just.

The Exchange of Quality—mine, for Wealth—theirs. They knew and I knew where the back-bone of the bargain lurked.   Believe me I paid down all I engaged to pay and delivered them just what all their life long they hungered in the hearts of them to gain—incorporation with nobility . . . for *that* they gave me *wealth.*

> " But when they came to try their gain, my gift,
>   Quit Rome and qualify for Arezzo, take
>   The tone of the new sphere that absorbed the old,
>   Put away gossip Jack and goody Joan,"

why they were deeply and bitterly disappointed. What they'd imagined the life of the great would be 'tis easy enough to sketch.   They began to sadly miss all the ways of the commons to which they had been used so many years and old Pietro longed for his loll on the pothouse settle, and he took it too.   It's all very well for a commoner to hear talk of a damask canopy and a coroneted coat-of-arms atop, but its quite another thing to sit beneath it, to bear poverty and privation for pride's sake.   A prince, now, could put up with, say, a dinner of chestnuts, and lightly toss the husks to boil the brazier, but a petty nature splits on rock of vulgar wants. . . . One dish at supper and a little wine and water had made a prince grin, but the citizen shrieked !   Pietro and Violante not only shrieked they made noisy protest and summoned the neighbourhood to attest the wrong . . . they were ' murdered, stoned, burned, drowned, hanged,'—then they broke away to tell the rest to Rome.   So much for them, so far.   Now for myself.   What did I expect when I married ?   What does any husband expect from his bride ?   Surely I was well within my rights in expecting loyalty and obedience, and an attempt to please me and settle down into my ways and those of the household. Instead what do I find ?   Was my wife inclined to keep the pact we'd made ?   Not she.   From the very beginning she broke it, and she published it to all the world, finding out, pretty quickly, that I was " a devil, and no man"

> " In four months' time, the time o' the parents' stay,
> Arezzo was aringing, bells in a blaze,
> With the unimaginable story rife
> I' the mouth of man, woman and child—to wit,
> My misdemeanour. First the lighter side,
> Ludicrous face of things,—how very poor
> The Franceschini had become at last,
> The meanness and the misery of each shift,
> To save a soldo, stretch and make ends meet."

Then a tale of my cruelty that exceeded Caligula's, to the good old couple, and worse than all the infamous lie that blisters my tongue to speak, that *I* set on my young brother, the priest, to solicit her departure from wifely fidelity !
Now I ask you, the Court, and my lord,—I said—What was it she married for, what was it she was counting on ? Someone said in answer " Love."—So, the Pompilia, child, girl, wife in one, wanted me to play the part of some country swain ! Beating pulse, rolling eye, frantic gesture, roses in shoe, plume in cap, trio of guitars at casement, and none knows what beside—me ! . . . Well, who knows under other conditions what I might have done ! It would have been for one of my own rank, though, that I can conceive it had even been possible for me to have rummaged these old odd corners of an empty heart for remnants of dim love, the long disused and dusty crumblings of romance ! But *this*, why this was just an ordinary marriage, with everyday conditions and no more. Pompilia was no gentle dove ; she was a hawk that I bought at a hawk's price and carried home to do hawk's service. But though I might have given her a hawk's training I was ever considerate. . . . The obligation I incurred with my hawk was just to practise mastery, prove my mastership :—Now very fairly marriage may be likened to the bond between

the Church and the monk.   How would my lords treat
and train a refractory monk ? I asked.   Suppose your
monk instead of taking penance rightly, with hue and
cry summons a mob to make a bonfire of the Convent,
say !—Well, it was in her way so,—and beyond the
so,—that my wife showed her insubordination.   You
follow me in my arguments, my friend ?—

Now my lords what think you was my next experience ?   Ah, but your lordships know ; did you not
adjudicate upon your knowledge ; yet had you been
able to mingle with that knowledge of the bare facts,
just the changing colours of my feelings who knows
what verdict you might have found intermixed in the
colours ?

Pietro and Violante having returned to Rome,
published before my lords, and spread abroad by print
and words that they had cheated me who cheated them.
They'd wound me through my pride of name.   My
wife, Pompilia, they declared was no true daughter of
theirs, but just the bastard babe of a drab and a rogue.
They had palmed her off on me, their story ran, as their
daughter with dowry.   Daughter ! Dirt o' the kennel !
Dowry ? Dust o' the street ! Nought more, nought
less, nought else but—oh—ah—assuredly A Franceschini and my very wife !

What did I do ? Did I fling Pompilia from me to
drop in the street, where such imposters die ? Nothing
of the kind.   I branded their statement false ; yet
even if it were true, I said, *she* is no party to the
fraud ; she suffers by the statement and is held up to
public infamy by their story.   This my argument.
Now clearly what was Pompilia's duty as my wife,
when Pietro and Violante swore her none of theirs ?
Was it not an overwhelming gratitude for my grace ?
—for was not mine an act of grace ?—give me this, my
lords !—At first, when she heard what her " parents "
were telling all over the place of her shameful birth,
she made confession to my brother the Abate, of what

the pair had counselled her against me, when they
should be gone. You bid me pause just here and re-
mind me of the false letter, and say that it was none of
hers, that she but traced the characters drawn first
by me ! But do you not see that granted so, by it I
but taught my wife her duty ? Is not the very christen-
ing of the inarticulate babe a similar act, a very saving
of the faith that else would perish unprofessed ? I,
—by this marital act,—put Pompilia in the way of
right-going. And she, who was reputed to have been
mothered in so foul a way, surely it would be only
natural to assume that such an one would be well
inclined to exaggerate chastity, to err in excess of
wifehood! But, my lords, what happened ? Just the
contrary, of course !
It was in the house, from the window ; in the church
from the hassock, that Pompilia still launched forth her
looks, letting looks reply as arrows to a challenge . . .
'Twas thus she filled a bitter cup for me, in which were
mingled gallant's praise, fop's reproach, minion's
prayer, and, at cup bottom, Caponsacchi ! I,—chin
deep in a marsh of misery . . . showing as the sole
unstrangled part of me my face, and 'tis there this
new gadfly attacks me, which I in turn must attack.
. . . You, my good lords, ask me to tell why I did not
try to rid myself of this last torment by mild exhorta-
tion. You taunt me that in my writhings in the mud
of misery I breathed out threatenings, rage and slaugh-
ter ! What you will ! It's all finished now and in spite
of my threatenings ! See fate's flare full on each face
of the dead guilty three !
I see now but too late, what a fool I was not to have
been summary with my wife at the first stray inclination. Too much talk ; too little do. Peter's way with
Malchus, kept Malchus quiet at any rate. Judas,
who received sops, after he'd been proved a thief, made
much ado in treacherous betrayal of Truth to cruci-
fixion, and later 'twas more than ear he lost ! I *did*

try the gentle course with her ! What was its end ?
Why, I was drugged, and when I woke it was to find
a crowd in my room, fumes in my brain, fire in my
throat, my wife gone God knows whither, rifled
vesture-chest, and ransacked money-coffer. " What
does it mean ? " The servants had been drugged too,
stared and yawned—" It must be that our lady has
eloped ! " " Whither and with whom ? "—" With
whom but the Canon's self ? One recognises Caponsacchi there ! "—Then was a babel tower of gossip with
core of " told-you-so, don't you know " reared about
mine ears. They the good neighbours all knew the
time, the persons and the play.—Bit by bit they fitted
together the pieces of the tesselated floor on which
devils danced and frolicked, around my broken gods,
over my desecrated hearth ! Well, this way I was
shaken wide awake, and after certain efforts with
medicines had been made to destroy the effects of the
drug I was set on horseback and bid seek the lost. I
set out alone . . . but all that story was told you, my
lords before, and, in this same chamber did I bare my
sores o' the soul and not the body . . . you know
your judgment. . . . The priest to Civita, just out
of the way ; my wife to Sisterhood,—and me ? . . .
to refund the moneys paid by Pietro, save the dowry.
Priest banished, wife immured, and pronounced no
daughter, but " a changling " ! Clear proof enough here
of guilt. Innocence is not banished ; purity is not
sent to the Convent of the Convertities. And I,
forsooth, the injured one, must pay back the sum !
I could not take back my name ; that part of the bargain stood. My lords, I ask was your judgment free
from blame ? I stand here to-day, who might not so
have stood, under this greater charge, on trial for my
life, and between me and my Maker the . . . dead . . .
those whom I killed and one . . . my wife, Pompilia
Franceschini !—But, harrassed, broken, troubled,
tortured as I was I played the man as best I could and

applied for a divorce. But no, my lords, Rome spoke
and told me that my plan for a divorce was all a mistake, and told me too " The Convent quiet preyed
upon your wife's health, she is now transferred to her
parents' house "—Mark that " parents " after the
Court's own decision ! And not alone this news the
Court communicated to me, but told me also that Paul,
my brother, my single prop and stay, Paul the faithful
servant of the Church, cut to the quick by ridicule of
Rome, the City, through my affairs, has sold off his
house and his goods and left Rome and gone whither
nobody knows.

Now I fancy my lords will expect that this moved
me to take such action as the human nature of me urged.
I recall a certain afternoon in autumn, when I'd received
that missive that told so much and meant more.
I walked home with it, mounted the stair and sat at last
in the sombre gallery. My poor old mother was in
bed, having to bear the cold the finer frame of her
daughter-in-law had found intolerable. My brother
was walking misery away o' the mountain side, with
dog and gun, belike. I supped, and as I ate the coarse
bread and drank the watered wine I strove to fortify
my mind, and said aloud, to strengthen the thought,
" Let me be a man, confront the worst of the truth,
end, and have peace ! . . . I am the last o' my line
which will not suffer any more."

Three months later came a new letter from Rome.
I even smiled as I received it. My mind was " made
up " and not to be ruffled by any letters, come they
from Rome or the land of Moab. " My brothers are
priests, and childless ; so that's well. And thank
God most for this, no child leave I ; none after me to
bear till his heart break the being a Franceschini
and my son ! " I read the letter. . . . " You have a
son and heir—'tis only eight months since your wife
left you, so the child *is* your son and heir. Now you
see the cause for quitting the Convent. The babe was

F

born last Wednesday in the villa of old Pietro and
Violante, who ushered you into life a bouncing boy, and
he's already hidden away and safe from any claim on
him you mean to make—(They need him for themselves, your bantling—your nerve laid bare—they
know how to nip it with finger nail)."

> " Then I rose up like fire, and fire-like roared.
> What, all is only beginning not ending now ? "

Whose babe ? How should it be called ? Franceschini,
Caponsacchi, which ? . . .

> " Say by some mad miracle of chance,
> Is he indeed my flesh and blood, this babe ?
> . . . The child I had died to see though in a dream ;
> The child I was bid strike out for, beat the wave
> And baffle the tide of troubles where I swam,
> So I might touch shore, lay down life at last,
> At the feet so dim and distant and divine
> Of the apparition as 'twere Mary's babe
> Had held, through night and storm the torch aloft,—
> Born now in very deed to bear this brand
> On forehead and curse me who could not save ? "

And all the time, believe me, friend, there was the
deep doubt in the heart of me, that the babe was none
of mine—but his—the priest's. My lords, I said, bear
with me . . . I show you the Hell around the Central
Heaven and both within me. The Hell : this bastard,
and the fraud of those that fathered it on me ; the
Heaven : that I was still alive, a man with brain, heart,
tongue and right hand too—No more of law ; a voice
beyond the law enters my heart,—who is for God—
are *you* on His side ?

I told the tale in my own Vittiano to my own serving
people—and each and all declared what he and they
in my place would have done to end priest, wife, and
ruler who offered no redress for such grievous wrongs !
I called out the first four resolute youngsters my glance
alighted on, to follow me, and donning the first rough

rural garb I found, and seizing any weapon that came
to hand, out we flung and on we ran or reeled Rome-
ward. . . . I've no memory of anything that happened
by the way, I found myself, as though I had been borne
on the wings of the winds, arrived at Rome on *Christmas
Eve*. The Christmas bells were ringing, everywhere.
It was the Feast o' the Babe. Joy upon earth, peace
and goodwill to man ! I started as the bells pealed
forth and let drop my dagger. Nine whole days did I
pause and pray to enter into no temptation more.
If you can just see that deserted house of my lost
brother's ; he had gone and with his flight had left it
desolate, the ghosts of old social joys mocking at me.
. . . For a time I would hear nothing, see nothing
but the face of the Holy Infant and the halo there.
By degrees the Babe's face vanished and only the Cross
stood at the end of all. The angels' song " Peace upon
Earth " was lost in the louder song " O Lord how long,
how long be unavenged ? "

Then scratching within my brain was slowly syllabled
" *One* more concession, one more decisive way and *but*
one to determine thee the truth." I took that way and
so found myself in the dark, before that villa, with my
friends. I knocked at the door. I made the final test
for truth. " Open," I cried. " To whom ? " " To
Caponsacchi," and the door opened. ———

And then,—why even then, I think and hope that
had but Pompilia's self, the tender thing who once was
good and pure, was once my lamb and lay in my
bosom, had the well-known shape fronted me in the
doorway—stood there faint with the recent pang,
perhaps of giving birth to what might, though by
miracle, seem my child—nay more I will even say if
that old fool Pietro had opened the door, I might have
paused. But it was *she*, the hag, she that brought hell
for a dowry with her to her husband's house. She,
the mock-mother, she that made the match and married
me to perdition. . . . Violante Comparini, she it was,

with the old grin amid the wrinkles yet, opened . . .
                         There was the end !
Then was I rapt away by the impulse, *one immeasurable
everlasting wave of a need, to abolish that detested life.*
'Twas done : You know the rest . . . how I was mad,
blind, stamped on all, the earthworms with the asp,
and ended so. . . . Absolve me then, for I have but
executed law's award ! Protect your own defender,—
save me, Sirs ! Give me my life, give me my liberty,
my good name and my civil rights again."
    It was thus dear friend I prayed them. I told them
that I'd plenty of use for that life ; I reminded them of
my good lady-mother and her age ; of the fugitive
brother who had so faithfully served the Church ; of
the spirit-broken-youth at home and I prayed give me
—for last best gift my son again, whom law makes
mine, . . . let me lift up his youth and innocence to
purify my palace, room by room. . . . then may we go
forward, face new times, the better day. . . . then will
I set my son at my right hand and tell his father's
story to this point, adding " the task seemed super-
human, still I dared and did it, trusting God and law.
. . . And if for answer he shall stoop to kiss my hand,
and then, suddenly remembering that it had shed blood,
drawback, or start, I shall smile, and explain, *That*
was an accident i' the necessary process, just a trip
o' the torture-irons in their search for truth,—hardly
misfortune, and no fault at all.
    I could speak no more. My brother has appealed
to the Pope, who has referred him back to the law, and
surely the Court in Truth's name can give but one
judgment ! What if you, good friend, were the Court !
How should I stand then ? Surely, surely 'twere
monstrous to make my life pay forfeit, that slew the
serpents that entangled it !

BOOK No. VI

" GIUSEPPE CAPONSACCHI "

BOOK No. VI

" GIUSEPPE CAPONSACCHI "

DEAR FRIEND,
  I think that when we stand in the Judgment at that
final time there will be *no words*. That sublime
Judgment will take effect without all the miserable
tangle of wrangle-jangle words ! We shall *know* ;
Truth, the Revealer, will make all things plain in a
flash of insight that will be outsight too. I, Giuseppe
Caponsacchi, priest and man and sinner, have had
flashed into my benighted soul the Truth, and its glory
and its purity have burned away all that kept invisible
The Holy One. In the Court, before the erring human
judges I tried to enmesh in the words of our common
speech, the tragedy of souls . . . the tragedy in which
She . . . and I have a part . . . or must it be " had "
for her, as she has passed from out the temple of her
fleshly body . . . and yet so slight flesh that as I will
tell you later, I *saw* the spirit through it.
  I was asked to " Come, counsel the Court in this
extremity." You remember, good friend, that six
months ago I appeared before the same Court, to tell
that for telling which I got that jocular piece of punishment from a then smirking, tittering Judge. It was a
grave enough Court this time. . . . No, not grave
enough . . . Were all the gravity of all grave men
who listen to the tales of human woes and sufferings,
condensed, until the atmosphere of Rome itself were
solid gravity, yet should there not be " grave enough "
for me. They stared aghast at me, these judges, as
though they were looking through a ghost ! I was no
" pert priest " this time ; I was " Friend " . . . I

told them of it ! I bade them mind that they laugh
longest who laugh last. . . . I reminded them that she
I had helped eight months since to escape her husband
had been retaken by him—though *they* were her
guardians—and butchered as she foretold and as myself
believed. I spoke . . . or my words came, or some
words came, maybe *not* mine, but I do remember that
from my mouth a voice issued which said to them
" My masters there's an old book, you should con,
for strange adventures, applicable yet 'tis stuffed with.
. . . Do you know there was once this thing : a
multitude of worthy folk took recreation, watched a
certain group of soldiery intent upon a game,—how
first they wrangled, but soon fell to play, threw
dice,—the best diversion in the world." There was
such a silence in the Court you might have heard a
feather floating on the air. And then, I know I leaned
forward, for I would have spoken in the ear of Judge
Tommati (he who smirked and smiled before) and said
" They *now* are casting lots, ay, with that gesture
quaint and cry uncouth, for the coat of One murdered
an hour ago ! . . . Pompilia is bleeding out her life,
belike, gasping away the latest breath of all, this
minute, while I talk—not while you laugh." Tommati
winced ; he's vulnerable . . . that's *good* for him.

This to me, I told them there, seems so strange that
you need any explanation of a deed of which you saw
the beginning, and knew, had you thought, must end
as now. *There's the fact* ! It seems to fill the universe
with sight and sound, and tells itself over from the four
corners of this earth, to my senses at least . . . but
you perhaps your need is that it should be set back,
as it were, that you may comprehend it the better.
Well then let me, the hollow rock, condense the voice
of the sea and wind, interpret you the mystery of this
murder. . . . *I* left Pompilia to your watch and ward,
and now you point me—there and thus she lies !
I wonder why you sent for me from Civita ? Was it

that you thought the occasion offered an opportunity
to free me from lock and ward ?

Thank you ! I am rehabilitated then, a very
reputable priest ! But she—the glory of life, the beauty
of the world, the splendour of heaven . . . is fast
dying (you tell me) while we talk, Pompilia,—how does
lenity to me remit one death-bed pang to her ? You
call me a fool for speaking so ? Say that I am providing
that base man, Guido, with an argument, one of his
dirty kind. But she, she was spotless . . . I too am
taintless . . . You can't think, men as you are, all of
you, but that, to hear thus suddenly such an end of
such a wonderful white soul . . . must shake me,
trouble and disadvantage. Sirs, *Only seventeen* ! But
I'll calm myself. Your indulgence allowed me to
speak for her or none might have spoken ; but now
to the point ; and I'll not stray again.

I am a priest. I certainly did not enter the church
as a bread and butter business ; to prove this it is only
necessary to say that I am a younger son of the oldest
and once the greatest House in Arezzo. I recognise
no equal there. First we were in Fiesole and later of
Florence, where our palace and our tower in the Old
Mercato attest this truth. This was nearly 400 years
ago. Our arms are those of Fiesole itself. The good
old Bishop, still living in Arezzo, my grand uncle on
the paternal side, was the one man who years since
prevailed with the Granduke Ferdinand to save the
city which he had sworn to destroy ! So you see there's
bishop in the family—in the blood. From infancy I
was predestined to the priesthood, and the day when I
was to read my priestly vows came soon enough. I
was by my vows to declare the world renounced. . . .
It was an awe-inspiring idea to me, and I pronounced
myself utterly unworthy, but the good Bishop smiled
at my misgivings, and explained to me that in these
latter days it was *not* necessary to prop the Church by
breaking my backbone as the necessary way *was*

once—to make buttress-work as did the martyrs and confessors. You'll be doing quite as much for the Church, in your day, as they did in their's if you march boldly up and take your stand where they died and cry "Take notice, I the young and free, and well to-do i' the world, *thus* leave the world, cast in my lot thus with no gay young world but the grand old Church : she tempts me, of the two ! " The Church has had enough of the offscouring of the earth ; we want the elegant, the scholar able to get at grips with society. You are just the man. . . . You need not *renounce* the world ; you must attract it and bring it us. Go on writing those beautiful verses of yours that attract the ladies . . . and then think of our gain when we shall be able to say " Yes and this talented young poet is ours . . . a living priest of Rome." So I became a priest. On those terms I could still hold up my head and yet walk as priest. I was a diligent priest along these lines. I wrote rhymes, was punctual to my place and diligent at my post, where beauty and fashion rule. I became sub-deacon, canon, and all went on well with me both in Society and in the Church. I was a *social* priest.

Three or four years passed in this way ; a pleasant kind of life, but of course quite unlike my old idea of what it meant to take the priestly vow !

I was at the theatre one night with a brother Canon, and in a theatre-mood, when there entered, stood, sat a lady, young, tall, beautiful, strange and sad. I looked at her . . . I stared at her . . . but no answering look was given me. Then my friend, the Canon Conti said, " I'll make her look at you," and without more ado he tossed a paper twist of comfits to her lap, then quickly dodged behind me, nodding from over my shoulder. Then she turned, looked our way and smiled the beautiful, sad, strange smile. He told me she was his new cousin, and that she had

married, three years previously, the old scape-grace,
Guido, lurking there in the black of the box. "I have
given up going to see them": he said, "I simply couldn't
stand it, seeing the wretchedness of the house, the poor
old Comparini couple crouching in fright each on each,
in a corner of the place, hardly daring to draw breath !
Look at Guido ! See how the black, mean small creature is frowning. Don't look at him ; look at her little
feet instead ! What a fool I was to fling the sweetmeats.
Be prudent, for God's sake, or the ill-natured husband
will make it hard for her ! To-morrow I'll try and make
things square again ; try if I can't find means to
take you there." My good sirs, all that night and
next day was I permeated, as by strong rays of light,
with the beautiful, sad, strange smile of Her.

At vespers Conti half said, half sung that he had seen
Guido, and mentioned my name, but that Guido had
seen me "staring" at her, and was in no mood to
receive me . . . adding we wouldn't care about him ;
he's no Hercules, why he'd lick your shoe, properly
managed, but it is the wife we must be careful about.
He beats her already. Poor little thing, she's breaking
her heart, as it is, quite fast enough, so you must be
rational and continue to please little Light-skirts
yonder. Every body knows what great dame she
makes jealous ! " Before a week had gone I made up
my mind about things, up to this point at least, that
I'd write no more canzonets, and I'd be in my place in
my Church,[1] S. Maria della Pieve. My patron spoke
abruptly to me, upbraiding me for being too close in
my attendance at Church and not going more into
Society. I told him I was going into Retreat instead,
in Rome, to look into my own heart a little, as I was
troubled in my mind and hard pressed by some novel
thoughts.

[1] This Church is said to be as old as the beginning of the 9th century. It
stands on the site of an ancient Temple of Bacchus.

Well, Sirs, shall I tell you how one evening in mid-
March twilight I was sitting musing, my book open
before me.   The musings ?   my life and how it had
seemed to have broken short, showing a gap between
what I would and what I was ; of the slipping of the
the soul into abyss ; of aspiration left here and achieve-
ment there ; of the weakness that failed to catch up the
ends ; of how dissociated my life was, for instance, from
that of the sad strange wife of Guido ;   of the stores
of strengths contained in me, eating into my heart for
want of employ, and yet, yet held from offering her
just the finger's help she needed—no way, none, by
which I might extend my help !—Shall I go on good
Sirs ?   I looked at my book, again ;   such a good book !
Its pages glowing with preaching, teaching, but in the
glow, in the text, between the lines what think you
most impressed me ?   Just her pure smile, as if to ask
" Any help for me, in its words . . . any direction how
to lift one finger-weight of my burden ? "
    There was a silence wrapt about me, not dull, nor
dead, nor cold, but a deep silence, when into it came a
tap, from the door without, and a whistling whisper . . .
" Speak up ; come in " I cried.   In glided a masked,
muffled mystery, and laid on my open book a letter
. . . stealthily laid it there. . . . then stood and
waited.   I took the letter ; its subtle atmosphere was
felt through every pore of me.   I knew before I read
it that 'twas a thing of evil.   But I let my eyes confirm my instinct and I read it.   Would you wish to
hear it again, Sirs ?   You've heard it once, but lest
you should forget—?   It was to this effect that she I
had lately flung the comfits to offered me in exchange
a warm heart, love and a meeting at a side door ; her
husband, the surly patch, being away at his Villa at
Vittiano.   " And you ? "—I asked of the messenger,
" What may you be ? "
    " Count Guido's *kind of maid*—Most of us have two

functions in his house. We all hate him, the lady
suffers much. . . . What answer may I take to cheer
the sweet Pompilia ? " Sirs, I wrote my answer,
wrote it to Guido's jealous self whose mean soul grinned
at me through the obvious trick. This is what Guido
read in the letter nominally for the lady :

" No more of this ! That you are fair, I know :
But other thoughts now occupy my mind.
I should not thus have played the insensible
Once on a time. What made you—may one ask—
Marry your hideous husband ? 'Twas a fault,
And now you taste the fruit of it. Farewell."

There, I said to myself, that's better than kicking his
messenger downstairs. *That* reply will make him
suffer ! In another mood I'd have kept the sham ap-
pointment for the gratification of cudgelling the
appointer, who was sheltering behind the gown of this
part-messenger, part-mistress.—But then, on that
evening, another mood was mine !

The morning brought a second letter, a precious
document indeed, upbraiding me with being cruel in
neglecting " Myrtilla " ; " Why is it you *dare not*
come ? " You must love someone else," and abjectly
offering, even if I loved two more, to gracefully accept
the crumbs vouchsafed to her as a third ! . . . " Are
you determinedly bent on Rome ? I am wretched here,
a monster tortures me ; carry me with you ! Come
and say you will ! Concert this very evening, do not
write, I am ever at the window of my room, over the
terrace, at the *Ave*. Come ! "

I read—questioned—lifting half the woman's mask
to let her smile loose. " So you gave my line to the
merry lady ? " And answer received of how she
treasured the letter, wept at evening when I did not
come and all night because I was not with her. She
had written the second letter; that the husband was
away, that I ran no risk, and that Myrtilla (Pompilia)

awaited me. So, I wrote a tantalising letter—a
second hell's worm for him—one that should cause the
chuckle at what he conceived as my inclination *to yield*.
Later he would lour at disappointment. Meantime I
would tantalise and enrage by turn . And so the mis-
sives followed thick and fast, for a month say, I still
came at every turn on the soft sly adder, endlong 'neath
my tread. Met in the street, signed to in the church ;
scribbled slips on the door-sill; 'twixt the pages of the
prayer book ; dropped before my feet ; pushed through
the blind as I passed the window, once a day, and ever
from corners his light-of-love, lackey of lies, would
peer up at me, always to chide me for being " still
obdurate." Ever the same answer she drew " Go your
ways, temptress, in the end you'll have your way and
ruin me."

One day a different style of letter was brought me.
It told me that I gained little by being timid. That
the Count had discovered Pompilia's love for me and
would stick at nothing to destroy me and advising me
to stand prepared or better still " run till you reach
Rome. Anyhow I beseech you stay away from the
window ! He might well be posted there."

You'd wish to hear my answer to this ? I wrote " Tell
him he owns the palace, *not the street under*,—that's his
and yours and mine alike ; and if this evening I choose
to walk there, well, if he like to put himself into a rage
over it he'll still have the trouble to put himself out of
the rage ! " And, I added,—just to keep his hell-worm
going—" Be cautious though at the *Ave* ! " Now
Sirs, when I gave this evidence before, someone smiled
a sneer, and asked " Why were you so confident that
these letters were from Guido and not from his wife ?
What if she'd written the letters ? "

I would as soon have believed that a live snake
of venom could have issued from the lips of Rafael's
Madonna's mouth as could these reptile emissions
from Pompilia ! But all the same these pestilent

letters and the black teazing lie for ever obtruded,
wearied me, . . . So I resolved I will go to the window,
as he tempts, . . . this adventure bait allures me, and
I began to laugh as I thought how I would hail him

> " Out of the hole you hide in, on to the front,
> Count Guido Franceschini, show yourself !
> Hear what a man thinks of a thing like you,
> And after take this foulness in your face ! "

The words lay living on my lip, I made the one turn
more—and there at the window stood, framed in its
black square length, with lamp in hand, Pompilia !
She looked as Our Lady of All the Sorrows, One
look she gave me, and vanished. They had used her
for a snare ! Again I would have called out Guido, but
all at once she re-appeared on the terrace above me,
and while I watched she bent down so close she could
almost touch my head. How full her tone was of
suffering, of tender reproach, of pleading, as she told
me that I, a priest, had dared to send to her, a wedded
wife, letters declaring my love to her ; she said that
she, herself, could neither read nor write, but that a
woman of Guido's household, read and " explained "
them to her ! " It cannot be you mean this wickedness " she said. . . . " But good true love would help
me now so much—You've offered me much money
because I'm in poverty and starve but I only want
enough to save my life. . . . Let me explain to you
how I am placed." And then she told me in such
moving terms, that I think that even inanimate, static
things must have thrilled at her poor story, of the
kind old " father " and " mother " lost ; of the dreadful change that had suddenly come into her life—without a word of say on her part,—when made Count
Guido's wife ; since when, all peace, all joy, all hope
had gone, and a nightmare of a dream had come ;—
those who had loved and cared for her for years as
her parents, had suddenly renounced her.—Could it

be, she questioned, because it seemed to them as if she were one with him who had so tortured them that they had fled ? She told how in her weakness and distress, and without one friend of her own, she had confided her poor little tale to Archbishop and Governor, and even to her Confessor, who had promised to write for her, as she herself could not write, to the Comparini and tell them of her sufferings, and how, in her utter misery, she feared that she would sin that sin that would take herself from off the unfriendly earth, unless they would fetch her or send for her, but that the letter, if he had ever written it, had never been answered, and she was in such dire trouble and bitter grief that she begged me to show that pity and mercy which I should show to a poor dumb dog, masterless, left for strangers to maltreat, and help her out of her surroundings, by taking her with me, to Rome to the Comparini. Still more she said. They had told her I had written those vile letters, they had " explained " them to her, and yet, she said " Now that you stand and I see your face, and look into your eyes that fearlessly meet mine, I know that you never wrote them or at any time intended to do me wrong. It is all false ; You are true and will be true to Rome—When is it you take me there ? Each minute lost is mortal. When ?— I ask."

I told her I would arrange it all—money and speedy means of travel to take her to her friends in Rome and that on the morrow at that hour I would pass.

Here, my friend, I bade the good Judges stop a moment and refer to the notes of the old trial. There they would find a subtle remark inserted. " You say Guido forged the letters, but don't you see that according to your own admission even if he did actually write them he only clothed the lady's meaning, the spirit of the letters, with a body, when he found for that meaning, words ? " " The fact is she herself solicited your help, and what men call ' loved ' you." But just as

sometimes the clouds pass over the face of the full
moon, and the moonlight streams through the clouds
and shows them up not as solid but as a kind of hazy
smoke, so, as I looked at the face of Pompilia, and into
her pure eyes, and caught something of the light of
innocence therefrom and saw it shine through the hell-
smoke of the faked letters attributed to her, I saw also,
by that same revealing light, that the smoke of the
letters which had purported to come from her to me,
interfused with that of the letters purporting to go
from me to her. As the hell-smoke drew aside I saw
my clear bright moon again. How then stood matters?
He had not only forged the words for her but words
for me, made letters he called mine : what I sent he
retained, gave these in place, all by the mistress
messenger. As when truth came into full power I
recognised Pompilia, so she, by the crystalline soul of
her, knew me,—never mistook the signs. Do you
attribute all this to thought ? Nay, sirs, it was *not*
due to thought. I've thought a deal and deeply, on
God and my duty to God, on my neighbour and duty
to him too, but this was not thought. !

   All night long I paced the city.

   Shall I tell you what really came to me ?

   Just as Spring rushes in as an invasion of Winter,
and behold all things are new, so it was with me. I
lay passive to an invasion so mighty that by it old
things were swept away ; abolished all that oppressed
me. Sirs, ye are " Masters " in the Church ! Know
ye not the meaning of the new birth ? Sirs, I was a new
man . . . to me had come the miracle . . . I was
" born again " ! I saw the Truth now ; . . . I won-
dered at the sight . . . death meant to spurn the
ground, to soar to the sky. . . . It was true that death
was the heart of life. . . . I saw too that all the harm
my folly had crouched to avoid was just a veil hiding
the very good, the gain that I would grasp. Oh Sirs,
that night and the wonder of it ! Scales from the eyes,

plugs from the ears, numbness from the feelings in a
trice were gone.   A new man stood erect. . . . and
through all the pangs of this birth I was thrilled with
an ecstasy that out-throbbed pain.

   As the grey dawn broke I saw again my familiar
Church, the Pieve.   Never had it so appealed to me.
It seemed to speak.   To claim me, to ask " But am
not I the Bride the mystic love o' the Lamb, who took
thy plighted troth, my priest, to fold thy warm heart
on my heart of stone and freeze thee nor unfasten
anymore ?   There are men who are not priests, bound
to me as thou, who may bestow their life blood to save
this fleshly woman.   Not in such tone before had the
Church spoken to me when day by day I had risen and
left her at the signal made me by some foolish fan.
But *now* the church changed tone—now, when it had
first come to me that *life* and *death* are means to an
end—that passion uses *both* when she is indisputable
mistress of the man whose form of worship is self-
sacrifice.   " Leave that passion of life and come be
dead with me ! " was now her behest.   Obedience was
strange to me—but this new thing that had been struck
into me by the look of the lady, made the command
authoritative That word was God's.   I had been lifted
up now to her level.   I said to myself we are together
now.   She spoke truly.   I am a priest.   I see that by
this way comes self-sacrifice and not by the other way,
for me.   I will pay the perfect sum, sit down and
silently obey.   So I went home, to my room.   I sat
stone still and the morning became noon, and noon
waned to evening, and as the sun set I opened my book
. . . across the white page blazed but one black name.
Vespers rang.   I thought of her waiting, counting the
minutes till I should come to tell her all was ready.
I told myself God who created her could also save her
without me, by miracle if need be.   I could pray for
her.   I did, going to my place in the Pieve.   Then I
went home, and sat in the dark, and meditated.   Sirs,

you would like to know on what, and how I meditated ?
It was on her and on what she would think and feel and
suffer.   If I could but be sure that she would know that
could I do her good, whether that good could be done
to her with God or apart from God, I would do it ; for
God forgives sin.   Then there came to me the hurtful
suggestion that she might attribute to fear my inaction.
Fear ?   Of what ?   The world ?   The Archbishop ?
Count Guido ?—*I* fear the sword of Guido ! Let God
who hates lies see to it that she does not believe a lie !
I prayed.   Again the morning found me.   I worked.
So the day wore through.   At evening I knew that
having achieved victory I must not neglect to offer
counsel and comfort, both as priest and friend to one
so sorely tried . . . bid her not despair, for that God
could help by other means.   I would advise her to
appeal straight to Him.   I went.   I found her standing,
for the second time, leaning over the terrace.   Again
she looked at me.   Then she spoke.   In a moment
my soul knew its true high duty ! She said " Why is it
you have suffered me to stay breaking my heart two
days more than was need.   Why delay help your own
heart yearns to give ?   You are still wishful to help
me ; you know my need, still through God's pity on me
there is time and one day more : . . shall I be saved
or no ? "   There was but one answer . . . the Apostle
Paul might safely have given it.   I told her where to
meet, in the dark of the next night.   " If I *can* but
find the way " she said, adding " But I *shall* find it."
And then she bade me " Go now."   I went and rapidly
I made all arrangements for carriage, swift horse and
driver.   I hurried back to my own house, for the last
time ;   saw the *Summa* open, and remembered that it
was another Thomas to him who wrote this book, that
had his faith strengthened by the gift of Our Lady's
girdle.   I too, good sirs, have seen a *lady* and hold
a grace.   I can't tell you how that night passed ;
I may meet it again in the Future.   When the morning

came I bade my servant provide me with a laic dress
and a sword. As the day wore I felt stronger and
stronger in my conviction that what I was doing was
mine to do,

> " Till at the dead between midnight and morn,
> There was I at the goal, before the gate,
> With a tune in the ears, low leading up to loud,
> A light in the eyes, faint that would soon be flare,
> Ever some spiritual witness new and new
> In faster frequence, crowding solitude
> To watch the way o' the warfare, till, at last
> When the ecstatic minute must bring birth,
> Began a whiteness in the distance, waxed
> Whiter and whiter, near grew and more near,
> Till it was she : there did Pompilia come :
> The *white* I saw shine through her *was her soul's*,
> Certainly, for the body was one black,
> Black from head down to foot."

She did not speak but just glided into the carriage.   I
said to the driver " Go by San Spirito to Rome ; drive
as if the road were on fire beneath—I take all risk "—
then I sprang in beside her, she and I alone, and so
began the flight through dark to light, through day and
night, again to night once more, on to the last dreadful
dawn of all.

Oh friend, it was just here that I was carried away,
out of myself, as I told the story of those memorable
minutes, when she moved, or spoke or looked, can you
wonder !   I wanted the Court to see *what* I saw and *as*
I saw it ?   I longed to make a mirror that should, for a
moment, reflect the pure soul of Pompilia, that they
might see.   I cried " Men, you must know that a man
gets drunk with truth stagnant inside him!"   And then
was wrung from me, " Oh, they've killed her, Sirs !
Can I be calm ? "

I partly recovered myself and recounted the in-
cidents of the journey, with her speeches, and left the
Court to judge ! *They* judge *her* ! The silence in the
carriage, each sitting as wait two martyrs somewhere

in a tomb for the last trump, fearless and safe. . . .
This is not *love*, Sirs, it is *faith*, implicit trust in God
who reigns and rules.   Once or twice she sighed softly.
As the morning light came I saw her look at me and I
answered her look " Saved, so far . . . we are now in
Assisi, on holy ground."   " How long is it since we
both left Arezzo ? " she asked.   " Years—and certain
hours beside." I answered.   Further on when we changed
horses I left the carriage and got her some bread
and wine and brought it her.   " Will this hinder
. . . does it detain to eat ? "   I told her " Not a
minute . . . they stay perforce . . . we shall get
there."   Then she told me that the pain had left her
soul so suddenly, it almost made her fear to be so free
of pain ! For many hours we sat in silence, when quite
abruptly and suddenly she asked me " Have you a
mother ? "   I answered, " She died when I was born."
" A sister then ? "   " No sister."   Once she asked me
" Does a man's strength sometimes make him unhappy
as a woman's weakness makes her ?   Does it not hurt
us women if a baby hides its face ; we weak women do
not like to be feared by little children or laughed at or
scowled on by strangers.   Has strength its drawbacks
so ? "

At eve we heard the *Angelus*, and she said " I told
you that I can neither read nor write . . . but you,
who are a priest, will you not read Gabriel's song, the
lesson and the little prayer to Raphael, for us travel-
lers ? "   And I read.

At Foligno, where we stopped, the people of the post
house brought lights, and the driver said " This time
to-morrow if all goes well, we arrive at Rome."   I
asked her, on this second night to alight and take a
rest even for an hour, as we were past pursuit.   I
would stand in the doorway and keep guard.   But her
whole face changed at my suggestion.   Misery about
the mouth, the eyes burned up from faintness.   She
reminded me of a poor hunted fawn, the huntsmen's

spear finding her, as she sinks tired to death in the
thicket. " Oh no, no stay ; on, on to Rome." And
all night we travelled on toward Rome. As the night
drew to a close she was troubled and restless and moaned
and talked in her sleep. I tell you Sirs, that once wide
awake, she waved away something ; at arms length ;
she said " Never again with you ! My soul is mine, my
body is my soul's. You and I are divided evermore in
soul and body : get you gone ! " Then I prayed—
in my whole life I had never prayed as I did then.
" Let God arise and all his enemies be scattered ! "
Then she slept. When she awoke I answered her first
look " Scarce twelve hours more then Rome, then
no more of the terrible journey." She said, wistfully,
" If it might but last. . . . with no dread to be here
and thus. . . . never to see a face nor hear a voice !
Yours is no voice ; you speak when you are dumb ;
nor face, I see it in the dark. I want no face nor voice
that change and grow unkind." *That* I liked. That
was the best thing she said. Then I begged her to
descend and take some rest. For a while she waited
at a roadside inn. I told the woman at the inn that
she was my sister, married and unhappy and asked the
woman to comfort her; and so I left them by the garden
wall. When I returned the woman's little black-eyed
child sat close to her knee, holding a bowl of milk, and
Pompilia was nursing the infant child which its mother
had placed on her lap. All this naturalness had done
good, and Pompilia looked up and smiled at me.
As we continued the journey she told me of her first
confession, and how she had asked the Confessor to tell
her what fault to confess and how he had said " but
you should bethink yourself : each human being needs
must have done wrong." And then she asked : " Will
you candidly, as a friend, tell me whether if I were
overtaken with sudden death, running away from my
husband and his home, should I be accounted to have
died in sin ? " She said her husband used to seem to

harm her ; that he practised cruelty with her, hoping
by her sufferings to inflict suffering on others. . . .
" Now friend—(yes, she called me ' friend ' on this
occasion) tell me . . . what have I done amiss ? "
The day wore on. Her restless eyes began to rove :
I could see she was fearing the foe that mine eyes could
not see : she wandered in her mind. Once she called
me " Gaetano ! "—that is not my name ; whose name?
I grew alarmed. I promised the driver more and yet
more to quicken his pace . . . lest that did not urge
him enough I threatened him. There was to be no
halting. I cried " Help us God whom the winds
carry ! " . . . On we went until I saw the old tower of
Castelnuovo . . . " Rome is the next stage . . . say
you are saved, sweet lady." I said to her. She was
sleeping as I spoke, and woke with a start and a scream.

> " Take me no farther, I should die :
> Stay here ! I have more life to
> Save than mine."

Then she swooned. We seemed safe : what was it
foreboded so ? You should have seen her, as motionless, breathless, pure and pale I carried her into the inn,
passing through the pitying group gathered there, and
laid her on a couch, in this deep sleep of exhaustion.
I had no choice in the matter. The people at the post
inn entreated me to let her stay the night with them.
All night long—how long it was !—I paced the passage
and kept watch. I listened. There was not a movement, not a sigh ; they told me " she sleeps, so sound."
But a great fear held me . . . I throbbed with it from
head to foot. I was in the shadow of a great woe, so
much so that when the first pretence of grey stole into
the black of night I made up my mind it was time to
start on our way again. While the sleepy grooms made
what haste they could in the dark of that early morn I
turned, to go and break her sleep, and there faced me
—*Count Guido* !—There he stood, posing as master,

took the field, encamped his rights, challenged the
world ; leering with new triumph, scowling with the
old malice, and part howled and part hissed out his
sneering infamies.

With him were the Commissary and his men.   I was
at once arrested, but you've heard all that before.
You know how he ordered the officers of the law " now
catch her."   Oh Sirs, I was near the throat of him
then !   What held me back ?   Just a touch of the
Molière spirit as the ludicrous lie was launched by
Guido as he claimed HER as *his own* !   He even em-
bellished his claim by the statement that she tried to
poison and plunder him and all the rest of it !   That
trap of the ludicrous caught me ;   just held me back a
moment too long, or the earth would have been the
cleaner by his being off it, and brighter, more of heaven
here by Pompilia's light of life yet shining in it.   " Let
me lead the way," I cried " I am priest, the privilege
may be accorded me.   You men o' the world, experts
in—' truth '—watch her face when she sees mine,
and find out guilt, if you can ! "   We reached her room,
there she lay, on the couch, as I had laid her, dead
asleep, wax-white, seraphic.   The snake hissed through
her husband's voice " Seize and bind ! "   In a moment
she stood erect, face to face with the infernal husband.
" Away from between me and hell " she cried, " I am
God's, whose knees I clasp—hence ! "   I tried to reach
her side ;   my arms were pinioned.   The rabble
thronged ;   " hearth," " home " and the " husband "
was the cry, and they took Guido's part, falling on me.
She saw, sprang at the sword which hung at his side ;
seized, drew, brandished it, " Die devil, in God's
name " she cried, but they closed round her, twelve to
one,—" the unmanly men, no woman-mother made."

The sword had been taken from her and she lay white
as the snow, but, disarmed as she was, her *word* sufficed
to spike the coward.   Then Guido began his search for
the gold, jewels, plate, money and clothes of which he

declared he had been robbed, but the " search " 'twas
only a cover that he might discover the amorous letters
he had only too much reason to know that he would
find. He lost his fear, and began to strut about,
snuffing and sniffing o' the stage of his exploit. I then
spoke to the officers of the law and said that I appealed
to Rome in my right of a priest. Being a Tuscan
noble I could have appealed to the Duke, but I preferred
the Church. There was no refusing my appeal. So
to Rome, with Pompilia, I was sent, and we occupied
separate cells in the same prison. I told my judges
then, what you, oh friend who know me so well could
swear to 'fore God's face, that I never touched Pompilia
with my finger tip, except to carry her to the couch,
that eve, and that, so sacredly as priests carry the vessels
of the Altar. I said I have told you all this once, turn
up the papers of the old trial and see if I now vary in
my statements. I need not have come here. I was
relegated to Civita when "Guido-with-the-right" hacked
her to pieces, she, who had only *you* to trust to, you and
Rome, . . . I come here, purely as a friend of the Court.
Scarcely need I now recall how we went through the
pack of stupid and impure banalities called " letters
about love "—The very desecration of that holy word
fills me with rage. Love is God for God is Love, and
what is there in those bestial whinings that has to
do with Love ? But back to Civita. There I was
studying verse, when suddenly, a thunderclap pealed
in my solitude, and I was caught up by the spirit, as in
a whirlwind, and brought here—into this very room—
where you used your scales so recently to mete out what
you thought was justice. Guido seized the scales
from your hands, and *himself* meted out *murder* to his
wife and those who cherished her through childhood !
  Now you want to hear my explanation ? (Here
friend I was ironical . . . but let that pass !) This is
the truth, I said, as God has shown it me. Guido
wished to drive *her* into overt sin and shame, would

slay Pompilia, body and soul and save himself, caught
in the mud made of his own tricks, cheats and lies.
He wrote the letters which in the name of me and her,
his mistress-messenger gave her and me, that so before
the world we two might appear guilty. The woman-
agent, reading the letters to Pompilia, who could not
read, put *her* sense into my words. . . . Then, in spite
of all this misrepresentation which was a part of the
devilish plot, God, once again, was greater than the
devil, and when we did meet, she and I, He willed that
the spark of truth should be struck from out our souls,
and we *understood* ! And, Sirs, I saw then, saw, as
though there were nothing else to see, that there is no
duty patent in the world, like daring try be good and
true myself, leaving the show of things to the Lord of
Show, and Prince o' the Power of the Air. Our very
flight proved our innocence. Why need thus to have
jeopardised our happiness if that lie were true, which
says I had access to her when I would ? If such were so,
what need to flee ?

One more point, I said, and I will cease.

Guido slays his wife against law, then deal with him,
as once you dealt with me who saved her against law.
I have done with being judged. If you say I was " in
love " unfrock me then, degrade and disgrace me. For
myself no matter . . . but for Pompilia—be advised,
build churches, go pray ! You will find me there,
I know, if you come,—and you will come, I know.
Friend, just here, I saw a judge weeping and it gladdened me . . . it showed me that at heart he was good
and true. . . . " It was just so," I said, " that She
helped me ! "

" As for Guido," I pleaded, " do not condemn him
to death. It were too merciful . . . too good. Leave
him to glide as a snake from off the face of things, slide
out of life, pushed by the general horror and the common hate to the ledge of things, clutching at anything
and everything that appears to have an honest form,

but all things of reason, order, decency and use shall
disengage themselves from his clutch, and seem to ask
him ' What, you are he then that *had Pompilia once,
and so forwent her ?* Take not up with us ! ' And
thus I see him at last meet Judas—cockatrice meets
basilisk !—both indissolubly bound in their one spot
out of the ken of God, or care of man, for ever and
evermore.
I was so carried out of myself, I fear—nay not
fear,—I own I was rash in what I said . . . I told
the Court so, and began again to speak of her good-
ness and innocence and purity when someone told
me " She is dead ! " I went on talking, talking all
the more; ah me, but if words could undo the done or
do the undone much had been changed. Yet even
though they could achieve nothing yet must I speak
in the great name of justice—for sure 'tis God—
I bade them, " See this ; if Guido could have escaped
after his triple murder, someone would have been
held guilty of the deed. Look at the direction in which
it points ! " I lost myself, again, just here, my friend.
. . . I know I asked the Court to make *a Pope* of the
friar who heard Pompilia's dying confession and
declared that he'd never shriven a soul " so sweet and
true and pure and beautiful." They tell me, those
who stood by me, that after that I said

" Sirs, I am quiet again . . . what's to move so much ?
Pompilia will be presently with God ;
I am, on earth, as good as out of it,
A relegated priest ; when exile ends
I mean to do my duty and live long.
She and I are mere strangers now ; but priests
Should study passion ; how else cure mankind,
Who come for help in passionate extremes ?
I do but play with an imagined life—
O great, just, good God ! Miserable me ! "

Friend, who so patiently read, whatever else my
tale lacks of the truth absolute, *yet that last line will
hold . . . is true . . .* therefore your prayers ! Adieu.

BOOK No. VII

" POMPILIA "

BOOK No. VII

" POMPILIA "

DEAR FRIEND,

All this time I have been dying ! You may say we are all doing that all the time. Yes, 'tis true, but the strong inflow of life is in normal times so much greater than the outflow that we scarcely notice anything but the inflow. This week's experience has reversed all that for me. I've been Pompilia. I'll try to tell you how I became that much sinned-against and sinless one, the child, for whom the money-grabbing commercial man and woman have no mercy. The child for whose sake Jesus immortalised a mill-stone !

Pompilia, at twelve years old—look at any bright, sweet innocent girl-child that you know, of that age— was sold, to a scoundrel, much as a dog might have been sold to a bully ! But that statement is *mine* and not Pompilia's.

A strange place, a deathbed ! I am on it ; it is here that the final testing of life is applied. I am on this bed. None speak unkindly now. The face and voice I so dreaded does not come. People are so good to me. I'm only just a week or two past seventeen years and five months. I *seem* to have been alive a long long time. Yet the Church register tells my age and—oh it's enough to make one laugh—a long string of names— all mine. I hope my darling little baby-boy will some day say them all, slowly and softly and then he'll wonder, as he says them, which name seemed most like me ! *His* name is Gaetano—I chose that because I thought a *new* Saint, as Gaetano is, would be able to look after him better. You see the old Saints have so

many many people to care for and so much to do !
Why, all my own five Saints couldn't stop me from
being slain, nor keep away all the strange black things
that have crowded into my life, until I *really* began to
wonder if it was all an awful dream—

I am so glad, so thankful to the dear God that my
dear dear little child was born before . . . this . . .
happened. . . . I think *if* he had not first been born
and Count Guido had killed him too, that God Himself,
would not easily have forgiven him that sin.   Now its
quite easy, because He has told me in my heart to
forgive and I do . . . I do.   God forgive him, I pray ;
God forgive us both. . . . God forgive Pietro and rest
his soul. . . . God forgive Violante and give her peace.
She never meant to do a big wrong.   She was thinking
of how to make me happy ; and Pietro he was always
good and kind.   Why, when I was a wee thing I
remember riding on his back, and how he romped, and
played the big giant with me ; and when I was ill
he was so gentle and tender.   They both loved me
so, and I loved them more than I can ever say, they
were just all I had.

And then there came that time, three years ago,
when Violante, and Pietro too, declared before some
judge and crowd of people who flocked to hear their
tale that I was *not* their child, nothing to them.   I
think of my baby-boy again, and I smile.   He's safe,
snug away,   I am sure someday he'll ask " What was
my mother like ? " and they may answer him " Like
girls of seventeen."—But it won't be quite true of me
. . . I look older than most girls of seventeen, who
titter and blush when boys speak to them.   He, my
son, must be told that I was called Pompilia, it sounds
an old name, full of story.   I did not think at first
how different was my life to that of other girls of my
years.   Tiptoe, tiptoe, came my strange troubles,
until they were all around me—they lay down when I
did, sat down with me and stood close, so close to me.

After that hard trouble when Pietro and Violante
disowned me, there came another. I had been told
that "husbands, love their wives"; mine was all
bitter hate to me ! Then people said that my friend,
God's priest who took his vows to God, *loved* me, like
other husbands, than Guido, love their wives, and then
when they saw him they shook their heads and said,
pityingly, "No wonder you love him ! " I heard one
day read out in the Public Court, such dreadful letters
—they called them "love-letters" and said the priest
had sent them to me and that I had sent some of them
to him. Why you know I couldn't write all those fine
words if I tried my best to do it. I was learning to
write because Count Guido wished me to do so. Everything in my life has been as strange as were some
things in my play in the days when I was a small child
and played with a neighbour's child at "make-believe."
I seem to have had things offered me, called mine,
and then when I went to touch them they were gone.
Even my baby-boy went like that, when I'd only had
him with me for three days. Oh his dear little head !
He looked such a little darling, I thought he would be
my very own ; but no ! They said my husband would
lay traps and catch him. My baby trapped ! Of
course I let him go! Oh, but he's safe now. Why if he'd
been with me on that awful night, six days ago—New
Year's Day—he would have been stiff and cold, by
now ; but now I think he's warm and smiles and feeds
and lives, and some day he will be grown great, and
strong and tall . . . My son !
    I'll tell you of that New Year's Eve and then the
day ! We were all sitting talking of my Gaetano . . .
I had been helped off my couch to creep down to the
fireside by Violante and Pietro—I must keep up the
old words, and call them " Mother " and " Father "—
had helped me there, and dear old father talked, and
told how he hoped to win his side against Count Guido,
and Mother said " Don't talk so much ; you'll make her

H

head ache, she's not strong enough yet awhile to listen to all that excitement." We were all so happy and friendly on that New Year's Eve ! Father went out to look round the churches, and when he came back it was snowing and so cold. Mother made up a big fire, and brought out a flask of wine, and we all thanked the Good God that we were away from Arezzo. Father talked about the church of San Giovanni, of the fold, the sheep as big as cats, and shepherds as big as small boys listening to the angel,—when "tap" "tap" at our door. We started. You know the rest ! And now, now the misery of it all and the danger, have gone . . . and now that I am dying, sorrow seems to look different, not like sorrow. . . . I wept when Sorrow looked at me before, but now I can just look back at her and see that she was *more* than grief. This great joy is mine, my little baby is safe, quite safe . . . and I am not in so very much pain. The strangeness that made life so troubling and bewildering is gone, and I see soft colours glowing in it . . . I wouldn't miss them. I always thought the evening-sky more beautiful than glare of day . . . its like that now—soft sunset colourings —I think being washed clean from sin, absolved now, makes me see clearer, better. I am quite calm and happy. I will talk presently again, to the nuns ; they shall know how all this trouble befell, they are kind, and God teaches them to comfort others.

I have had so much more of happiness in life, than misery. Until my marriage every day and all day long I was happy. Now if it hadn't been so I think I might not have felt the change so keenly. One day my mother told me that on the morrow she would bring a cavalier whom I must permit to kiss my hand, and that that same evening he would be at San Lorenzo and marry me, and that when the marriage was over I should come back home with her, just as though we had never been to the Church. She said that I must not talk about it . . . girl-brides never did, as if my father heard he would be very shocked and, I should see him blush. I know that when she told me this I saw no more sense in it than a lamb does in people clipping wool; I lay down and let myself be clipped. I was surprised when the " cavalier " turned out to be old Guido Franceschini. I thought him like an owl that boys use for catching small birds. He looked worse when he smiled, but I thought little of him, as little as I should think of whether the coin which I took to shop was old and dirty or new and clean. It would get for me the thing I wanted. So the " marriage " with the old " cavalier " would bring me the praise of those I loved ! I knowing nothing of what a husband meant thought one man as good as another to serve as such, and Guido's ugliness did not trouble me. I remembered an ugly doctor who once cured me of illness, and people spoke of him as very clever. They did not say that of the other doctor who was good to look on.

It was a dull wet day in December when my mother took me, all cloaked and covered up " from the rain " into San Lorenzo. The church was very dark. Up at the Altar were two shivering candles. No light and warmth as usual. I thought at first I was going to look on a corpse—then I saw a strange priest, not our priest, standing out in the dull light. I learnt to know afterwards that he was Guido's brother, Paul. Then, from behind the altar out came Owl-face—and caught my hand. I didn't like to pull it away ; I let it stay for fear of being discourteous. I looked at mother. Her eyes were full of tears and her cheeks were very white. The priest read here and read there, and told me to say some words after him, and then when I had obeyed he said I was " a wife "—greatly honoured by being made one, as 'tis in this way that Christ weds the Church, to show that I should obey my husband as the Church obeys Christ. I felt very frightened I couldn't speak, I was too scared. My mother was weeping so, I hugged up to her to try and comfort her. When we got to our house door she said " Now darling, mind, not one word to your father. Remember girl-brides never breathe a word." So when he opened the door, and asked us why we'd been to church in such pouring weather (although the rain was stopped as we came home) mother gave my hand a timely squeeze and Madonna saved me from immodest speech. I kissed him and was quiet, being a bride.

Three weeks went by ; I saw nothing of Guido " Nor the Church sees Christ " I thought. I was " married " and I expected all was over. The ugly doctor had left when I was cured ; the ugly Guido had left when I was married and so nothing was changed. One morning I was busy with my broidery frame . . . the pattern went wrong and I was puzzling over the stitchery, when I heard loud voices, two or three together and sobbings. I quickly left the broidery frame, and ran to see what was the matter. There was the priest who had married me to Guido and old Guido himself and Pietro my good father who was looking very angry and his face was red ; he was speaking very quickly and indignantly. He said to my mother " You have murdered us and the child too ! " and she sobbed out " All of us murdered and its too late now. O my sin, O my secret ! " Then I grew afraid. I felt that something mean and underhand had been done ; it had to do with me. When father saw me he said " Go away my innocent lamb and pray God help thee." And I went, and prayed God ; and mother came with eyes all swollen and red. She told me to sit down beside her and said that she had planned everything to make us all as happy as might be ; that father was not so angry now that he understood better her intentions, which carried out gave me a husband and a noble name, a palace and no end of pleasant things. She said young men are changeable, but Count Guido is just the right man to keep the house ; that we should all still be together ; we should leave Rome for Arezzo, and live in a beautiful palace, and there I should be Queen, and she and father would see me honoured. Then poor mother's eyes filled with tears again, and she stroked my hand and said, " So my darling you will forgive me, will you not ? " and then she sobbed and sobbed. I told her she was wise and knew everything ; that I was only just a silly girl, a child and knew so little . . . that all was right, quite right, if only she would stop weeping. And so she dried her eyes and led me in to father, who was leaning, opposite Guido, and Paul said, as I entered " Count Guido, take your lawful wife until death part you ! "

All since has been a blank, a terrific dream, only dreams vanish when you wake and see the wholesome homely things in the daylight. I know I wake now, but from what ? It is all blank. Even the Confessor, Don Celestine, who tried for my soul's sake to help me wake my memory of the past the better to forgive it, tried in vain. He thought I could not properly forgive, unless I *remembered* what I had to forgive. I think things over, and as I think and some things come back to me, a light other than my life-light shows me that I've little to forgive at last. I must be fair and say my husband was ill-used and cheated of his hope to get enriched by marriage. Father and mother promised money with me, but they gave me and no money and so broke the bargain, and he became aggrieved and in his aggravation was unkind to me, to punish them. They said he began deception first, but was that any reason they should answer ill with ill, for so the echoes never die away ! If I *had* but seen, but I was blind, or had my sight been clear I might have persuaded my parents to give the dowry, and Guido to desist his hard treatment. Guido accused me of flirting, of sending love-looks at theatre and church, walking and at the window. I knew, of course I knew, that this was not true, but

what I did not know was why he charged me falsely
. . . what he tried to drive me to do. How could I
know ? Thus in my ignorance I made things worse by
never going out at all. When Guido's messenger began
to tell me of the priest and the letters they said he had
written to me I begged her to ask him to write no more
and not even to pass in the street where we lived. But
I think my greatest trouble came to me when Guido
demanded that I should yield him all myself. I felt
that there was just one thing he had no right to take
nor I to give, we being in estrangement soul from soul.
Remember I was barely twelve years old at marriage.
I told you that for weeks I was let alone, lived my child-
life, still. Can I make you understand ; it is difficult
to speak of these things, but I was told that Christ
loved his Church, his bride, and died for her, and
passing through death, yet lives for her . . . that in
love, by love, through love, He is *one* with her. Love
unites, Love makes two one, but awful union that of
flesh alone, of flesh where soul is apart from soul. Perfect love casts out fear and shame which torment ;
but Guido and I did not love and yet he came to me
and told me, angrily, that we had been man and wife
six months, and dwelt apart. " It must cease, to-
night," he said, " go to my chamber, not your own,
have done with separate rooms ; separate hearts is
another tale altogether." This awful word came to me
and I rushed from the house when I heard it and flung
myself before the Archbishop. I clung to his feet and
pleaded with him that for pity's sake he would forbid
what my estranged soul refused to bear, and place me in
a convent. " You bid me imitate the Virgin " I
cried. What was his answer ? " Folly of ignorance !
That which was glory in the Mother of God had been
damnable in the Mother of men, Eve, to whom her
Maker had said " Be fruitful, multiply and replenish
the Earth." Besides, he said, " 'Twas in your coven-
ant ! "—Then he smiled, but there was something in

that smile that caused my heart to sink. Then I told
him—for he might hear as God—Ah, but as if he
could !—a frightful thing, to prove that Count Guido
was seeking this unholy thing because he hated me and
wished to humiliate me, and not because he loved
me.—Holy Sir, I cried, if he loved me would he let
his own brother, the idle young priest, Canon Girolamo,
teach me what depraved and misnamed love means,
and what outward signs denote the sin. He solicits
me and says he loves me, and my husband sees and
knows it and lets be ! The Archbishop was impatient
of my story and imploring words. He told me a parable
of a fig that refused to be eaten by a bird, and so was
devoured instead by three hundred thousand bees and
wasps, and said that this should teach me to go home
and embrace my husband quick, and let his brother
see it, which would cause the brother to go back to his
priestly duties, and then the Archbishop sent me home
to the palace in his carriage. Oh but I know, my heart
knows now as it felt then, that he was wrong, so wrong !
    The worst befell me at home. My husband's hatred
did not change. His brother's boldness grew effrontery
soon, and I, oh I had lost, by force, my last stay and
comfort in myself, my very soul was desecrate ! The
taunting things that were said ; my mother's name
(my own mother, not Violante) was held up to me in
scorn, it was no wonder I was bad who had had such
a mother ! But I understand her better now. Maybe
that since what they called " love " was hate, what
they termed " hate " was love, and perhaps my mother
when she what they call " sold " me, her child, hoped
in her poor heart that I at least might try to be good
and pure, and so she'd save me from her life, who maybe
had no chance. Since so many things in my life meant
for my good seem to have worked me harm instead,
may not you, my mother, seeming as you harmed me
most, have meant to do me most good when you sacri-
ficed your babe and gave away your heart's hope, as I

might give my babe, loving it as you, if . . . but that never could be asked of me ! That makes me happy as I think of my babe ! He is mine only . . . I give him to God, by my death. I give him outright to God . . . to no parent in the world. What guardianship could be safer ? But I tire you all listening as you are so patiently, and understanding, I am sure. Four days ago when I was sound and well you would have misunderstood, as you did my friend, whom you called my lover, not seeing the glory of his nature, which to me shot itself out in white light and blazed the truth through every atom of his act with me. Oh you all imputed to him such wrong motives ! I must try, in these last minutes, to remove the stain some of your talk has made on his reputation, so that when I am gone and sorrow stays, and people need assurance in their doubt if God yet have a servant, man a friend, the weak a saviour and the vile a foe,—let him be present by the name invoked,

Giuseppe–Marie Caponsacchi !

Already the mention of that name has made me feel stronger. For his sake I'll cease forgetting the sorrow ; he lives and he is belied. If he could be here now how he would speak for me !

I had been three miserable years in that gloomy Arezzo Palace when I was taken by my husband to the theatre. I had no idea why, but I was sure that it was not because he loved me and wished to see me happy. I was soon to know his reason. Such a sea of faces ! Such a stare as if all the people's sight were concentrated in a single gaze ; such a buzz, as if all found the need to speak, in low tones, at once. On the stage two were singing " True life is only love, love only bliss, I love thee, thee I love ! " I saw them embrace, but to me the sight was painful—I turned away. I remembered the old festa days when I was a child—those dear glad days ! How often had I been puzzled to hear my parents say on such days, " You

will outlive us, it would be our joy to know that a pro-
tecting friend could shield you from all life's hard
things, and love you, when we ourselves have gone."
Sudden I saw that friend : my soul could make no
mistake ; I knew him for what he was, noble and good
and true. As I looked into his kind grave face I felt
his strength calming me and wished that I had such
strength to rest me in.

A silly twist of comfits was tossed into my lap ; it
came from his direction, but I knew that whoever flung
it was not he. Then I saw the round good-natured face
of Conti, my husband's cousin, and I understood at
once, who had done it ! Conti came over to us and
laughingly said " Cousin, I threw them hard to make
you look as austere as Caponsacchi, yonder." My
husband heard, and frowned, and at supper time he got
in a rage and drew his sword and pretended to thrust me,
telling me I was a wanton, and that my amour was the
town's talk, and he threatened revenge on Caponsacchi.
All I said was " It is untrue ; God save the innocent,"
and I went to bed, and praying, slept.

About a week later Margherita, called my waiting-
maid but more than a servant to her lord, the Count,
began to tell me of the priest's danger, and of his love
for me and begged me to warn him to be on his guard
against my husband, and she besought me to send him
the token of a glove. I bade her be quiet, and never
again mention the subject to me. But the next night
she began telling me how she'd seen Caponsacchi and
asked him to desist : that he had entreated her to bring
me just one little word he wrote. " I know you cannot
read," she said, " therefore let me ! This is what he
says, only two words ' My Idol.' " Her importunity
was great. I told her that though she might continue
to bring letters purporting to be from Caponsacchi,
until they were countless, never would I believe that
they came from him. I had seen his face, and as well
might I mistake the face of the devil for that of God as

believe that the portrait drawn by others of my friend
was true.

April was half through. I had gone to bed as usual
caring little whether I ever woke again, when I was
wakened at daybreak—the light was vivid, wondrous, a
broad yellow sunbeam reaching from heaven to earth
and it seemed to me as though it were a beauteous
drawbridge, from my prison to the freedom and glory
of all things. The spirit of the Spring tripped over it
and invited me to trip too. The dewdrops, the dancing
insects, the building birds all were finding life good and
oh, strange miracle, my heart sang too in response to all
this chorus-twitter of happiness. Rome! Rome! They
are all gong to Rome, the Easter ended everyone leaves
for Rome. Caponsacchi too, as well as the Archbishop,
was off to Rome. *I* would go. I would get away,
somehow! How often I had tried to leave Arezzo,
to put an end to the wicked life with Guido who so
hated me and loathed me that he never lost an opportunity of degrading me to make me loathsome to
myself. God pity and the Virgin help all poor girls
married without love! There is no desecration, no
degradation so awful. Now it seemed to me that this
spring-time I would get away, in spite of the Archbishop, the Governor, Guido and all. I would implore
Caponsacchi to take pity on me and to help me, by
showing me just enough friendliness to escort me to
Rome, to those my parents who had loved me and so
cared for me in days past. It was my husband's cousin,
Conti, who had at first suggested to me that there was
no other way to free myself from Guido and from sin,
than by escape, and none who would dare help me to
escape save " my fellow-Canon, brother-priest, Caponsacchi." He said " He's your true St. George to slay
the monster." Well, the first thought on waking,
that beautiful morning of spring was just that suggestion of Cousin Conti's. Who should come into my
room, quite early on that particular morning, but

Margherita whom I detested. She began chiding me
for never having given a thought to Caponsacchi, who
she said, had stood all night, like a sentry, beneath my
window. I suddenly stopped her with a " Tell Caponsacchi he may come ! " She was gratified. I saw
that look on her face that told me this was her heart's
desire. But she said " You've so often spurned him,
perhaps he won't come now." I answered " Say to
him that After the Ave Maria at first dark I will be
standing on the terrace." Off she went saying " May
he not refuse, that's all, fearing a trick, mayhap a
flower-pot dropped on his head." I answered " He
will come." Oh how I prayed ! It was a day of prayer
to God the Strong, the beneficent, to put forth His
might and save me.

When the dusk came, the dark, I was pushed as it
were by the spirit moving me, out on to the terrace and
there was the silent and solemn face of my strong
deliverer. This precious time, this chance and yet so
much more than mere chance, was mine. I told my
friend " I am in course of being put to death . . . for
a long time this has been going on, but while it only
concerned me I put up with it as best I could, but now
I imperil something that's trulier me than this myself :
something I trust in God and you to save. Take me
with you to Rome and put me back among my own
people."

He replied, and put deep feeling into the answer,
moved by my peril and sufferings, " I am yours."
A night passed and he did not come to tell me how he
would arrange. The *second* night he came. How
many prayers had I put up since last I saw him ?
Just one, for I never ceased praying. He said " I've
thought much of what is best to do but the plan is
impracticable and for your sake I dare not venture it."
I told him that the risk was to him not to me, and I
asked him " *When* is it you will come ? " " To-
morrow at break of dawn," he said, and directed me

where to go. That night, my husband telling me how
he loathed me, bade me beware that I disturb him not
as he slept. " Couch beside me like the corpse I would
you were ! " he said.

The rest you know I think, how I found Caponsacchi,
and escaped. Some of you who listen to me are
inclined, perhaps to think, even if you do not say as
much, that my friend's great effort failed, after all,
seeing that I am here. You are in error. I will not
admit for a single moment that that great service
failed. I say, the angel saved me : *I am safe.* He
did more, he saved my babe. If I had stayed in
Arezzo, in all that noise and trouble he would have gone
back to God, and I should never have seen him. The
sweet peace and the love that surrounded me all the
months before my baby's birth, restored my soul.
All has been right ; I have gained my gain, enjoyed as
well as suffered, and had a foretaste of a better life
beginning where this ends.—No more strange cold looks
were bestowed on me during my time of weakness ;
I lay in the arms of love, till my boy was born. Oh
that fortnight ; it was one of bliss—All women are
not mothers of a boy, though they live twice the length
of my whole life, and, as they fancy, happily all the
same. That last Christmas too ! I had never realized
God's birth before.

My father and mother they too are safe—they see
God. As for Guido, who still draws breath of life, I
pardon him ? So far as lies in me I give him for his
good the life he takes. . . . Let him make *God* amends
—none, none to me, who thank him that at last he has,
even in this way, blotted out the marriage bond. We
shall not meet, he and I, in this world or the next. If
Guido stands out of the light let him touch the shadow
of God and be healed ! He hated me so, and now that
he will no longer see the one he loathed perhaps his
heart will feel less bitter. *I* could not love him but his
mother did. His soul has never lain beside my soul ;

—his very touch had polluted that body he has des-
troyed, and so after all by his " destruction " saved *me*,
as by fire.

My little babe, God's orphan, thrown into His arms
from birth ! I will not think of my child as Guido's,
only as mine, born of love, not hate, I give my little
one quite to God, to His Fatherhood.

Let my *last* words be for my *one* friend, my only
and my own, that put his breast between the spears
and me. O lover of my life, O soldier-saint, No work
begun shall ever pause for death ! Death shall not
separate us. In the new path I have to walk in that
life beyond the grave, I will walk it with my weak hand
in his strong grasp. But he knows ! Tell him I never
doubted that he would have been with me now if the
world had not held him back. Tell him that I am
arrayed for death in all the deathless flowers of what he
said and did. He is a priest and cannot marry, nor
would he if he could, the true marriage is that of heaven,
where those who love *know* themselves into *one*.

> " So let him wait God's instant men call years ;
> Meantime hold hard by truth and his great soul,
> Do out the duty ! Through such souls alone
> God stooping shows sufficient of His light
> For us i' the dark to rise by. And I rise."

BOOK   No.   VIII

"DOMINUS   HYACINTHUS   DE   ARCHANGELIS
PAUPERUM   PROCURATOR"

BOOK No. VIII

"DOMINUS HYACINTHUS DE ARCHANGELIS
PAUPERUM PROCURATOR"

My Dear Friend,

I wish you could have seen my ruddy rogue
"Cinone" on his eighth birthday ! Luck, that carries
a man over a ditch if he can jump well, carried me over
the difficulties of as interesting a law study as I have
ever engaged in. Curly pate's birthday too ;
why in the name of that same Luck weren't you at
supper with us ? My dear friend you cannot rightly
estimate what you missed. I'm a family man ; have
long since settled to my own satisfaction that if a man
would make the best of life he must early find a good
woman and ask her to share it with him. When the
children come along the man begins to feel and realise
that he is alive, and that that " good " woman is now
" best." You should have seen my help-mate ! I
told her that the biggest " case " I had ever argued
had come to me to work up on Hyacinth's birthday and
I took it as a signal proof that there's a special providence for fatherhood : I tell you what, my friend, my
fatherhood has given a flavour to my law. I was never
so keen to match blades with Fisc before. I want this
" eloquence "—don't laugh !—I repeat it, this eloquence of mine to be remembered when Cinuolo-boy
becomes a man—when he comes of age. By great Jove
it will, too ! My life is bound up with that boy of
mine ! I pity you, friend, from my heart's heart that
you've so much opinion of the bachelor state that you
don't care to change it for the family state. You

I

really *should* have been with us at the yearly lovesome frolic feast of the little lad's.   There's just one reason why I can afford, after all, to let poor old Bottinius score a point or two—he's a bachelor—I, as a married man and a father, know what he misses.   He only prides himself on what he avoids.

The birthday feast was memorable ; while it was preparing I worked at double speed, and the flavour of the feast improved the flavour of my arguments.   By the by do you know that the Cardinal, my very good friend has promised me that he'll personally read my speech to the Pope's Holiness—and he'll point out the—flowers—and the bays, too.   I'll tell you, when I hear, what the wise Pope says of it.

But do bethink you, my dear friend, what a piece of downright good fortune has come my way.   Here have I a *noble* to defend ; indeed it is too much luck to befall me, on Giacinto's birthday too ! Not only have I a noble to defend but one who with mighty parade killed three very well-known persons.   I can tell you simple truth when I say that during that festal evening, before the supper, while I was preparing my " speech," I kept thanking God for the opportunity and asking Him to keep my head from swelling.   I determined to make my defence of Guido of such a kind that it should be fit tribute to my wonderful boy— fact ! I do call him wonderful—so would you, if you knew him as I do, and he were yours !—Do you say you would like to know what I considered a fit supper for the occasion ? I rub my hands now as I think of it. It was good, done to a nicety, too.—Well, we had wine, minced herbs, fennel and parsley and liver, goose-foot and cock's comb, cemented with cheese ; roast porcu- pine, and jugged rabbit.—But the flavourings ! My cook exceeded herself.   Now, don't you regret your absence ? I can't send you the supper, but I can send you my pleas.   Here they are.   Read, mark, learn and inwardly digest these arguments and let me have

your comments. I've been particular with the Latin.
Should like to have brought in Virgil, but it wouldn't
have been quite the thing in prose, would it ? As you'll
see I have dealt with the case in earnest. Really the
whole thing will be decided on much broader lines.
Still, law must have its say. All the time I was working
up my points I saw that fellow, Bottinius, in his study,
working against me, preparing thrusts that will be hard
to parry, and introducing all those surprises, which
method makes his manner. I couldn't help thinking,
as I laboured, and the delightful aromas of the birthday feast mingled with my breath, of poor old Guido on
that bitter cold day, in his straw-strewn dungeon, hell
in his heart,—a frozen hell I'll be bound. He married
too late in life, and then married a young creature, who
made his years tell against him and brought him into
ridicule. What a poor, skinny, miserable entity he
is ! Scarcely a drop of good blood left in his veins, I
should say. He looks starved in more ways than one.
The best and most manly thing he ever did, I presume,
was to risk his own wretched life by that triple murder.
You wouldn't think to look at him that he had the spirit
of a mouse. Upon my word, friend, I'd have given
him a dish at supper, for Giacinto's sake, and in honour
of the boy's birthday, if only he'd been near enough !
It's a queer thing to what specimens one's sympathy
runs out !

But here's my address ; what think you of it ?

MOST ILLUSTRIOUS, THE JUDGES—

We shall first of all demonstrate that Honour is a
gift of God to man precious beyond compare. This
honour is as naturally sensitive as the pupil of the
eye. If but a gesture threaten to touch it immediately
ire is called forth. . . . As the pupil of the eye is to
the eyeball so is the honour of the wife to the husband.
Revenge of injury done here, to the honour proved the
life and soul of us, cannot be too excessive, too extrava-

gant. Such wrong seeks, and must have, complete revenge. I could quote authorities galore in support of my statement.

Theodoric the Goth, King of Italy 493–526 as quoted by his secretary Cassiodorus, when propounding the basis of the household law ends his argument something like this. " Bird mates with bird beast genders with his like and brooks no interference." . . . Bird and beast ? . . . He needn't have ended there. The very insects are on the side of our argument—Let Aristotle doubt. The bees, for instance ; the epithet of *castoe apes* signifies THE CHASTE. They never hesitate what to do when their honour is offended ; they sting the offender to death ! If a poor animal, a negligible insect, thus feel honour's smart, taught direct by Nature's instinct, shall man,—Creation's master-stroke—man of the nature of the Judges here, prove insensible, the block, the blot o' the earth he crawls on to disgrace ?

Right away from primitive pagan times, when the half-lights shone on man, the breach of the marriage vow required, demanded, the penalty of blood, blood alone being able to absolve the outraged husband, who, anticipating law, himself drew the sword,—down to these Christian times—to St. Jerome himself, who writes to show that honour injured, there follows contempt or indignation . . . that either lowers the mind, casting it down from its lofty heights by reason of disquietude.—Under the smart of outraged honour, the place, the memory of the shame, the scorn, urge a man's spirit to such a fury that it becomes a delirium of frenzy. Nothing can satiate the man's spirit, nothing can hold him back from his just revenge ! Think you any of the little rules of propriety, the fear of shame, or loss of dignity can deter him ? What does Saint Bernard say in his epistle to his nephew ?

" Too much grief does not excogitate propriety nor knows shame at all, nor consults reason, nor dreads the loss of dignity ; order and the mode it ignores."

Surely we have here the painting, the very portrait
of the distraught husband, Guido Franceschini !—
If we take the highest authority of the Christian, our
Lord Himself—we find that he suffered opprobrium,
contumely, buffetings, without complaint ; but when
He found himself touched in His honour, never so
lightly for once, then outbroke His indignation, before
pent up, and He cried : "No, My Honour I to nobody
will give."
Revelation, old and new, admits that

> " The natural man may effervesce in ire,
>   O'erflood earth, o'erfroth heaven with rage
>   At the first puncture to his self-respect."

Just consider, my lords, how things stand now.   Under
Moses the Law allowed the *stoning to death* of the
adulterous wife.   " Stone her not ; put her away "
legislates our Lord.   Last of all comes the Church and
tears away the divorce-bill that the Gospel grants :—
What then is left the outraged husband ?
PRIMITIVE REVENGE !—Society's dictum is this :—
Unless the husband will appear floridly infamous,
vile and of indescribable turpitude, he shall with his
own hands straightway take revenge rather than appeal
to a Court.—My Lords, if the motive prompting a
husband's revenge be injured honour, and he fail not,
straight away, to avenge it the Law imputes NO BLAME.
    I could pass before your lordships many instances
where the punishment awarded by the Court to those
who have taken the Law into their own hands and
committed murder, has not been for the murder committed but because the *mode* chosen by the avenger
has been at fault.
    History is full of examples which doubtless your
lordships will remember without detailed citation.
But there is NO SINGLE INSTANCE of any man, taking
the Law into his own hands to avenge his honour,
meeting with Law's buffet solely on this account.   If

his mode of procedure were right, his motive single and straight—the cleansing of his honour—the means to this Lawful end were held Lawful by the Law. That the murder of Pompilia was attended by aggravations is incontestable ; YET my lords, these aggravations are but as parasite growth upon murder's back. If the murder, admitted by Count Guido Franceschini be allowed as the exercise of right and healthy instinct of the mind, approved by nature, primitive times, Christian times, our Lord Himself, and by the society of to-day, what becomes of it as CRIME ? If there be NO CRIME how then can these " aggravations of crime " stand ?

Guido, the husband, gentleman and Christian was, in honour bound to avenge his honour.

If, my lords, it be urged that Guido allowed time to elapse between the time he discovered his wife with the priest at the inn of Castelnuovo and his later act, my answer is clear and convincing. Thus :—I contend that no time was lost. Look at the circumstances adverse to Guido's promptitude of execution ! When he arrives at the inn the priest is there and flourishes his sword ; the wife, like a fury, flings herself on her husband, the crowd are swayed by the " lovers " ; then follow the capture ; the appeal to Rome, the journey, the second journey to the shelter of the house of the Convertites, the visits to the villa, and so forth :— There was not one minute left us all this while to put in execution—*the revenge planned o' the instant !*

It is true that, Rome reached on Christmas Eve, Guido allowed the Christmas week to pass before he sought vengeance. But we must allow for some religion, even in these heterodox days, some care for the Feast of the Holy Church, some merest charity this Christmas time ! Nor, during that week's interval are we able to picture Guido, the outraged husband, at rest. We regard him as raging here and raving there—We can hear him saying as he paces the rooms :

" Money I need not friends I have none ; what I ache
and hunger and burn for is that the WHITE be restored
to my shield, that shield borne aloft on great occasions
by my race, by my own grandsire who fought as a
hero ! " . . .

Guido, of the line of the illustrious Franceschini,
suffered torments, tortures, in the interval, and short-
ened it to its least moment possible, all things taken
into account.

There is no PAST in dishonour. He who suffers as
Guido suffers has always in his mind and heart the
unhealable, inflammatory wound.

Wound the body and soon the smart mends and
ends. Wound the honour and the soul where honour
sits and rules, and the longer the sufferance the stronger
grows the pain. Dishonour of the marriage vow is ever
present ; it knows no PAST. . . . Time cannot blot
it out.

My lords I have shown that Count Guido's action was
not delayed, and the injury, the hurt to his honour,
was not of the PAST but admittedly of that type and
class of injury which is *ever present*, while life lasts, in
noble hearts.

Nor is the slaying of Pietro and Violante the crime it
appears at first sight to be, since they were not two
good parents—even by adoption—but having thrown
off all sort of decency had renounced Pompilia, declaring her the offspring of a drab, just that so Guido, who
had made her his wife, might lose his social rank !

He killed the clan " lest longer life might trail link
by link his turpitude, hateful so to kith and kindred."

And he killed them here, *in Rome*, here in the Eternal
City, Sirs, where Lucretia's self slew herself to wash
away the spots that she as victim was forced to receive ;
here, in Rome, where Virginius killed chaste Virginia
his daughter, to keep her chaste. . . . Here, Guido
killed them all three, in their *own abode*, that each
wretch might both see and say " There's no place nor

yet refuge of escape shall serve as bar to the one wounded in honour " ; killed them on the spot, moreover, dreading lest within those walls the opproprium be prolonged and the domicile which witnessed crime watch punishment also.—In other words Pietro and Violante who inspired Pompilia's conduct against Guido, and suggested that she should drug her husband and escape with the priest, should not survive Pompilia's death ; should not live to enjoy the dowry they had escheated from him ; should not live to point to him as a murderer ; should swallow their own lies with the death–swallow and should even in that supreme, that LAST moment, know that to a Franceschini nobleman HONOUR COMES BEFORE ALL THINGS.

There's my speech, done at last ! It's unanswerable. Some day, when my curly Cinone is a man, he will FEEL its beauty, see its lucidity and own proudly— " It was my father's work."

Now into the pigeon hole with it ; off and away, first work, then play, play, play.

> " BOTTINI, burn thy books, thou blazing ass !
> Sing, ' Tra-la-la, lambkins, we must live ! ' "

BOOK No. IX

"JURIS DOCTOR JOHANNES-BAPTISTA BOTTINIUS"

BOOK No. IX

" JURIS DOCTOR JOHANNES BAPTISTA BOTTINIUS[1] "

DEAR FRIEND OF MUCH PATIENCE,

If that little room of mine could but utter what I
have confided to it, if its four walls, moved by my
eloquence, should one day give forth the sounds likely
stored up within them, then might even the deaf adder
acquire hearing. But this business of writing is as
dull as a flowerless plant. Flowers of speech indeed !
They are mildewed or blighted by the time one is able
to gather them from the dead page. But this little
room of mine, poor little place that it is, you should
see the fine audiences it sometimes contains ! Judges,
lawyers, the elite in letters, and as for me I address
them all ; bowing now on this side now on that ;
pausing ; then with slow and clear enunciation and
marshalling the facts in due order, I present my arguments, quite unanswerable, I assure you, by which, do
I seek to prove guilt innocence, or innocence guilt,
I succeed most convincingly. With me the great art
of the matter is always to end on a note of interrogation.
Do you follow me ? Having proved the " pro " the
thing is to immediately follow the proof by asking,
" But if the ' con,' just for argument's sake, be admitted what of us ? See its interpretation ?" And so
whichever way the judgment goes I'm right . . . I'm
the man of wisdom . . . he who has seen the points.

Archangeli, of the swinish appetite, is a family man ;
as for me, as you well know, my mind is not set that way.
But that is not to say that I don't understand the
weaker sex. Why I could sketch you a standard

---

[1] Bottinius was Public Prosecutor.

maiden.   Ages since God standardised all the girls.   **He** gave them interchangeable minds, interchangeable manners, interchangeable words.   One maiden can speak for the lot.   They are as like as two peas in pod, two lambs in a flock.   Why bless my soul the world is full of Pompilias.

And yet this particular Pompilia became quite another creature, almost another species, after her marriage.   The fact is, my friend, I couldn't paint her, though I studied all her lineaments separately, each for a whole month.   She's elusive ;   she's sufficiently elusive to evade that common clay, Archangeli, who can more easily see feasts (such as he took care to sit down to a few evenings since) . . . he can't see character, not he !   It is true that Pompilia eludes me, but I *know* that she does so.   I see enough of her to realise that.   Archangeli, on the other hand, blunders along in his clumsy way and thinks he's got her there, and is showing her to the public, with all the clap trap " love letters " " discovered " by Guido, when she's no more captured than would be the rainbow, if he opened and closed his hands on the colours !

As I've said, and you know very well, I'm a bachelor, and as such know the entire gamut of woman's wiles— isn't it bachelors they're " nice " to ?   Caponsacchi, he's a bachelor, and a priest.   He knows all that's worth knowing of the standard maiden—and probably of the standard wife and widow too.   How many " confessions " has he heard, suppose you ?   Now having this knowledge how is it likely that he would be so great a fool and so benighted a priest, as to let a woman—maid or married—stand in his light—a man that some day might have been Pope ?   For my part I cannot for the life of me, see how Guido Franceschini can have acted as he did except on the understanding that he's of unsound mind.

Injured honour indeed !   Injured humbug !   Injured dowry ;   injured fortune ;   but if you'd care to follow my arguments you'll find them here set down. Try and imagine them declaimed before an immense hall full of people, as they should be if I had my way.

" MOST ILLUSTRIOUS THE JUDGES—

Since the chief defence of Count Franceschini the Accused, as we have heard from his Advocate, consists in the pretended plea of injured honour, by which he was moved to crime, it is my office to disclose the lack of foundation for this plea, in order that this atrocious and *enormous* crime may be punished with the due penalty.

It is not my intention to put before you by word-painting, feature by feature, outward frame and flesh of the maiden, Pompilia.

It is not so, my lords, that our famous artists have made their appeal. It is true that they make their numerous studies of a subject, but these they keep to themselves, using them to assist in producing the finished work. Less distinct is part by part, but, on the whole, truer to the subject—the main central truth and soul of the picture . . . a spirit-birth, conceived of flesh ; truth rare and real, not transcripts, fact and false . . . the studies of the separate parts that are to compose the whole picture are for students, but the finished picture,—the result of this careful study of individual parts,—is for the world. I, too, might begin in a similar way. I might even set out to paint for you the entire family group—Pietro, with his wise old wife (as if one introduced St. Anne by bold conjecture to complete the group) and juvenile Pompilia with her babe, who seeking safety in the wilderness were all surprised by Herod, while outstretched in sleep, beneath a palm tree by a spring, and killed,— the very circumstance I paint, moving the pity and terror of my lords.—

BUT I shall NOT choose this method. For a month past I have searched out, pried into and pressed the meaning forth of every piece of evidence in point.

By part and part I clutch my case and present it to you in its entirety, as I am sure you will agree as we progress. I shall not weary you with a parade of my studies, fifty in a row, as it were, but, bowing low shall proffer my picture's self. I shall, moreover, leave the family group and stick to just one portrait, but Life-size.

I invite you, my lords, to BEHOLD POMPILIA ! . . .

I do not intend to ask you to behold her as infant, child, maid, woman, wife, but I dare the epic plunge and begin at once with MARRIAGE.

There is no doubt that Pompilia, the maiden, was beautiful. Anacreon admits that Nature, while endowing MAN with STRENGTH, armed weak WOMAN with BEAUTY. The prerogative of beauty, its intimate essential character may be found in melting wiles, deliciousest deceits, the whole redoubted armoury of love.

Pompilia was a beautiful maiden ! WHAT THEN ? We shall not pry into her behaviour as a beautiful maiden but shall the wiselier wink at this and pass on to the time when marriage made it necessary for her to cry " Loves, farewell ! Let love, the sole (the only) remain." Henceforth marriage made, it is GUIDO'S privilege to guide Pompilia's step and cry " No more friskings o'er the foodful glebe, Else 'ware the whip." We can even hear the first crack of the thong which debars the young wife from the old free life. Nor is he, as husband, to be blamed for exercising his rightful authority over his wife. Pompilia must not be permitted to escape her wifely bearing, duties, pieties. Yet, my lords, bear in mind that patience is ever needed at such transit time when old things go and new arrive. Impatience in a husband *then* may well be regarded as silly and absurd.

We see that Guido, by his methods soon drives away Pompilia's people. He and she being left together alone in the house surely he may now feel satisfied that the old things have vanished, the old manner of life gone, together with the obstacles to peace, and that all is new and promises well. Or, if we quote Virgil we may say "Every storm is laid." We may also expect each pleasant flower to peep forth from the plain and that each bloom of wifehood hitherto in abeyance may now flourish . . . Keeping to this figure suppose that as with plants so with Pompilia. . . . Plants, be they never so well and carefully pruned have a way of springing forth and spreading here, there and everywhere, permitting other than the gardener who laboured with them to pluck them, lending their beauty to chance wayfarers ! . . . .

It is alleged by foes of the lady, that just so was she as free to everyone, besides her lord. Her charms were spread for all.

Yet I would plead that it is this universality, the very want of particularity in the bestowal of her favours that renders them—renders this bestowal—harmless. She chose NONE of all the admirers of her youth and beauty ; she gave to none the right to say " I was preferred to GUIDO." No butterfly of the wide air dare brag as much. That so many admired her did not detract in the least from her value to her husband ; the fact of this tribute to her of general admiration should the rather have enhanced her value to him. BUT for argument's sake we will even concede to Guido that the lady's charms were seen and admitted by too many and that from this point of view there was reason in his wrong. . . . WHAT THEN ? Pompilia submits to his will and before three years have passed, she puts away the reproach of lavish bounty ; no longer is Guido able to say, " she NONE EXCLUDES "—since " she laudably sees all, Searches out the best and selects the same."

Is Guido any fairer to her ? Does he show his implicit faith in this dutiful young wife ? Not he ! It is true that the man she selects as a friend is a priest, a friend of Conti, a relative of her husband, well born, well

cultured, young and vigorous, no miscreant singled
from the mob, but a man of mark !
Does Guido behave himself well over this ? Not he.
Old man as he is the faith of early days is gone. . .
Nothing has died in him save courtesy, good sense
and proper trust, Which when they ebb from souls
they should o'erflow, Discover stub, weed, sludge and
ugliness.—
Deserted by each charitable wave, Guido, left
high and dry, shows jealous now !
He avouches his jealousy, parades it, would make it
the excuse for all his small unkindnesses. If you tax
him with them he responds :—

> " Truly I beat my wife through jealousy.
> Imprisoned her, and punished otherwise,
> Being jealous : now would threaten, sword in hand
> Now manage to mix poison in her sight
> And so forth."

Well, this jealousy being admitted, Guido himself not
only admitting it but advancing it as a palliative for his
conduct, what remains to prove ?

> " Have I to teach my masters (the judges) what effect
> Hath jealousy, and how, befooling men,
> It makes false true, abuses eye and ear,
> Turns mere mist adamantine, loads with sound
> Silence, and into void and vacancy
> Crowds a whole phalanx of conspiring foes ? "

Therefore who own " I watched with jealousy my wife "
adds " For no reason in the world ! "
What need that thus proved MADMAN, he remarks,
" The thing I thought a serpent proved an eel " ? . . .
Such lunacy announced you must prepare that things
proceed from bad to worse. Threat succeeds threat,
blow redoubles blow, until there is at last awakened
in the wretched, wrongly suspected and ill-treated young
wife, a rebellion against this tyranny, say sooner, a
rising of self-defence, a laudable wish to live and see

good days. . . . By any means at any price, Pompilia
will fly this cruel fool, she will save him from himself
from what may be the dire result of his continued ill
usage of her—the double loss of herself and his unborn
child ! She must at all hazards stop the crime that she
knows Guido will commit if she does not escape from
him.—How can she escape ? Who is there that will
help her ? Who will dare displease Guido ?

Her sole weapon is her BEAUTY . . . her womanliness.
She thinks, at this crisis in her life of her friend, her
ONE friend, the priest. . . . He is almost a stranger to
her. . . . How shall she so appeal to him as to ensure
his help ? Can you, my lords, rightly blame our poor
Pompilia if circumstances compel her to use the arts
that allure, the magic nod and wink, the witchery of
gesture, spell and word, whereby the likelier to enlist
this friend, yea, stranger, as a champion on her side ?
You must remember that she had but a single friend
in the wide world, who might, as she thought help her
in this her dire extremity. WHAT, could she do other
than resort to him ? Often her hopes flag. How can
she bid him, whom she knows so slightly, brave danger,
disgrace, nay death in her behalf ?—His manly mind,
like stern steel requires, she fancies, love's lodestone. . .
Yet he is a priest . . . and wicked . . . if he break
his vow :—

Shall HE dare *love* who may be POPE one day ?

These are a few of the points I would make if you
admit the letters which Guido professed to find and
fix upon Pompilia and the priest.—For argument's
sake we will stretch our belief to allow that Pompilia
did write the letters. That in her loneliness and hunger
after friendship, she learnt to read and write ! WHAT
THEN ?

In one of the letters she tells how her life is not worth
an hour's purchase ; that she has but one hope of
safety . . . that he, the priest, is her only hope.—
What other can she offer him than love ? . . .

K

Money, diamonds ! . . . What would they be to him ?

POMPILIA'S SUPREME MOTIVE THROUGH IT ALL IS THE SALVATION OF HER UNBORN BABE. To secure this she will, if there be no way else, feign love and allurement. Does not the classic story tell how Venus, losing Cupid, allowably promised in the anxiety of her motherhood, " To him who shall tell me where my winged babe has wandered I give for reward a nectared kiss ; but to whom brings safely back the truant's self I give a super-sweet, makes kiss seem cold."

To such motive them refer all Pompilia's professions to Caponsacchi, the priest. She is accused of having drugged her husband and robbed him, to achieve her end. The accusation is a lie, yet were it truth she were but taking the most ordinary precautions to make her journey a success. How gladly would Pompilia have opened the door widely and fled boldly, but since Guido is what he is she must for his own sake as well as for her own, find means for flight, in masquerade. It is an hour when all things sleep, save Jealousy, and Guido is lying duly dosed and sound asleep, relieved of woes, or real or raved about. But the story of the drugging is a fable, a lie. . . . Yet were it true I would treat it thus. Softly she leaves his side. He shall not wake, nor shall he stop her as she steals away to join her friend, nor do the friend mischief, should he catch him, nor get his own head smashed.

The fiction that she stole Guido's money for her journey were it fact, would crtainly not reveal a crime, such as that of common robbery. Was ever husband's money better destined ?

As the first flush of the enterprise passes, and the priest has time to evolve incipient scruples and perhaps to regret all that he has undertaken, and to grow moody, cloudy, silent, as he contemplates his possible ruin, Pompilia's wit is heavily taxed to find a ready remedy. Say, what more natural than that she, seeing all that he was enduring, facing, risking for her salvation's sake, should kiss him and he being not less than man, respond ? . . . Whatever her conduct in her tragic trouble may have been, it is marked by this much success—it kept the priest her servant, to the end.

A day, a night, and yet another day they have been travelling, and Rome is but one stage away. They are surely saved ! Pluck up heart ye pair and forward then ! The admonition comes too late ! Pompilia, overcome by the hardship of the long trying journey following the many anxious months preceding it, swoons, and is carried out of the vehicle by Caponsacchi and laid to rest on the only spare bed that the inn of Castelnuovo affords. The poor, tired child, she is little more, sleeps all night, and Caponsacchi dreading the worst, waits in the inn porch, ready for any summons yet wishful not to break in on her sleep unless safety compel. She swoons and sleeps all night. Almost before the morning light, and while the night mists yet prevail, her chamber door is rudely and suddenly burst open and there dashes in a ribald crowd, led by her husband. Outcries and lewd laughter, scurril gibe and ribald jest, and Guido's indecent wrath, cause the poor, weary, but alarmed girl to spring to her feet and confront the foe. Pure as the sea, with a tide of pent up emotion rising within her, she seizes the sword of him who would slay her and their unborn child, and turns it against him ! At the flourish of the sword, even in a woman's hand, the crowd draws back and stands aghast.

"She looks not like a conscience-stricken sinner caught in the act, but like a poor hard-pressed all-bewildered thing," says one. Opposed by six she is quickly disarmed. The officers of the Commissary pinion the arms of Caponsacchi the priest. Pompilia sees him standing helpless before superior physical force ; she hears him say boldly to Guido, " What have I done ? I interposed to save your wife from death, yourself from shame." Passionately Pompilia takes up the tale, and denounces Guido in language that carries those present with her, and she hears as the result of her story mutterings of " Hands off, pay a priest respect," " persecuting fiend " and " martyred saint."

" I appeal to Rome,". . . " and I," say priest and wife. To Rome they all go.

You will perceive, my lords, that Guido failed on this occasion to avenge his honour to the utmost, but contented himself with overtaking the couple at the inn and publicly insulting them leaving it to Rome to pronounce law.

Law pronounces sentence thus—the priest to three years banishment to think things over ; Pompilia to the holy Convent of the Convertites, and Guido to pay the costs and await what ? . . . The multiplication of the jealous furies within.

This coward, Guido, who dared nothing ; who sought by all means public and private to besmirch his wife that any tales she might tell of him should be discredited, who failed to stand up like a man to Caponsacchi, and later, urged by the devils within to an unclean fury, set aside the law he had invoked and with vehement truculence assaulted his innocent wife,— the mother of his child,—and her parents, his vile perfidy using the door-key of Caponsacchi's name to gain admittance on that memorable Christmas, *this* Guido is now on trial for triple MURDER ! . . . But I anticipate, . . . At the end of five months the Convent's self made application that Pompilia might leave the house for her health's sake, that she might be allowed to go to the home of her parents and there get the fresh air her pale face asked, and the nursing that so soon would be required when the babe should be born . . . the said home to be regarded as the law's place of safety.

Six weeks slip and she is domiciled in house and home as though she had never left it. To Guido Franceschini there is born a son and heir . . . true sum of all earthly good. . . .

Now, if ever, is Guido's chance ! Joyous, contrite, quick, hasten, Guido, to thy wife, the mother of thy son ! But how shall GUIDO banish from his breast the apparition . . . the phantom that to him is real ? He who has yielded the ground of his heart to the entertainment of all unclean and loathsome creatures ! . . . He hears a whisper . . . a voice . . . from the bogs of his unclean fen . . . " 'Tis said that when the nights are lone and company is rare the priest's visits brighten up the winter."

Fool, Fool, Fool Guido to listen !

The priest has never once left his relegation-place ; there is proof abounding to any but a mind so warped to truth as thine ! But suppose that it WERE TRUE that Caponsacchi stole a visit once and again. Yet he was lonely too ! What great harm if he should in presence of her parents and herself discuss the details of the tragic journey ?

Return O husband ! Put away from thee thy stubborn heart and find thine arms of fatherhood and take unto thyself that present which thy generous wife bestows on thee, her too parsimonious lord. She will not let the old year go without that precious gift ! Oh nothing doubt. In wedlock born law holds baseness impossible !

Ah, but the demons of doubt are riding thee husband to a fall ! The babe's name, my lords, is neither from the sire presumptive nor the sire potential, neither Guido, nor Guiseppe—but GAETANO—Last saint of our hierarchy and newest namer for a thing so new.

Guido's heart and mind have no room for the little child this Christmas tide. The devil drives . . . the reins are out of Guido's hands now ! But my lords, you know the rest ; it is before the Court.—

To the last Pompilia played her part ; used the right
means to the permissible end.

> " And wily as an eel that stirs the mud
> Thick overhead, so baffling spearman's thrust,
> She, while he stabbed her, simulated death,
> Delayed, for his sake, the catastrophe,
> Obtained herself a respite, four days' grace
> Whereby she told her story to the world,
> Enabled me to make the present speech,
> And by a full confession saved her soul."

Do I credit her last story ? No.
Do I think she lied ? Equally NO.
I account for it this way :—
Pompilia was at the point of death, and statement
made at that point passes with the church for honest
and sincere statement. If then she was sure that
whatever she said would be believed, it was but charity
to spend her last breath in one effort more for the good
of both friend and foe. By pretending to utter innocence she reintegrated not only her own fame but that
of the priest, her friend.

If her confession could persuade her husband that
he slew a saint who sinned not, even where she might
have sinned, why it would but urge him all the brisklier
to repent, as it would cut away from beneath him even
the plank of CAUSE for jealousy. Yet, last of all, if
you are not willing, my lords to entertain kindly this
suggestion, liking not the genial falsehood, well then,
as a last resource, we will fall back on the inexpugnable,
submitting, she confessed before she talked ! The
sacrament obliterates the sin. . . .

Under the just torment of the vigil the accused has
confessed to the murder of the three. There remains
but one thing for him—JUSTICE—and that JUSTICE
demands that the only punishment commensurate
with the awful crime against God and man be inflicted
in expiation of the crime.

Guido Franceschini's LIFE to LAW is forfeit !

There's my oration.—

Much exceeds in length
That famed panegyric of Isocrates,
They say it took him fifteen years to pen.
But all these ancients could say anything !
He put in just what rushed into his head
While I shall have to prune and pare and print.
This comes of being born in modern times,
With priests for auditory.   Still it pays.

I shall watch Arcangeli squirm !   Wonder if it will
interfere with his appetite for supper—the pig !

BOOK No. X

THE POPE

BOOK No. X

My Dear Friend,

This has been a tremendous week for me ! I've been no less a person than that grand old thinker, Pope Innocent the Twelfth, and I feel more than eighty-six years of age ! Into this week many long years have been pressed, laid one on the other and with the weight of things pressed flat.

The Court found Guido guilty—and the rest—but by a subterfuge passed the final sentence on to me to send five souls to just precede my own, to bear witness, may be, how I did God's work on earth.

As the Pope I sat me down in my small plain room, furnished with a stool and a table and a crucifix. All the company I had with me there, my thoughts. I stayed within the little room all day. I read ; I noted ; I mused ; I referred again and yet again to the Lives of my predecessors, and in the chronicles I read of their judgments. I asked myself " Have I to dare ? How dared such and such of my predecessors ? To suffer ? How suffered another ? To judge ? How judged yet another Pope ? " I turned the pages o'er and o'er, to find their glory or their blots.

I saw what happened in Rome eight hundred years behind me, when one Pope blessed what the other had cursed, and then I asked myself which of the judgments was infallible ? As I watched them of old time carry the dead body of Formosus through the great door of the Church, and place it upright on St. Peter's Chair, reclothed in the pontific vesture after having been buried eight months. I saw as I

looked upon that frightful corpse-face that it was that
of Guido ; he was waiting . . . waiting my sentence.
I see him now, this Guido, this poor weak trembling
human wretch, pushed by his fellows who pretend
the right, up to the edge of a gulf dividing this
world from the next. There he stands on the edge
of the precipice, looking down with terror on the black
waters and entreating me to save him from a fall, to
conserve to him, the short space of time the natural
minute more. I hear the angry and indignant cries
of the avengers " Man be just, nor let the felon boast
he went scot free ; put him to death, punish him now ;
as for his weal or woe hereafter, God grant mercy."

What is before me, but to judge, weigh well and
decide either to hold out the saving hand, or to with-
draw my hold and let the wretch drift to the fall ?
Myself I die a thousand deaths, and stand as many
times before the unerring Judgment Seat of God !
My mind is well made up. I know of no doubt to
clear. Guido and his four confederates are guilty ;
he is chief of the guilty five. Presently the brief word
will be written, the handbell I shall chink, but now—
though I am resolute, and my mind as firmly fixed
as yonder mound with the pine trees on it, yet,—for a
little time, I'll pause and review intent the little seeds of
act, the tree—the thought, to clothe in deed, and give the
world my judgment, at chink of bell and push of arrased
door. Suppose it should some day be proved that my
judgment of Guido was erroneous, suppose acuter wit,
in days to come, should find him guiltless, I should not
blench in facing Guido's ghost but say " God who set
me to judge thee, meted out so much of judging
faculty, no more : ask Him if I was slack in use there-
of ! " Why, I should blame myself imputing a heavier
fault for having on one occasion changed a chaplain,
because he annoyed me by an unpleasant habit of
snuffling at mass ! You are surprised ? But consider !
" It is the *seed* of act, God holds appraising in his

hollow palm, not act grown great thence on the world
below, leafage and branchage, vulgar eyes admire.
Therefore I stand on my integrity, nor fear at all."
    It has been a wretchedly dull grey gloomy day of
advancing March ; the pouring rain has cleared the
streets of gossipry—but wherever men are gathered,
in their homes, or under archways and portico, two
names now snap and flash from mouth to mouth, the
names of *Guido* and the *Pope*.
    Suppose it were possible to compute by probability
tables, such as a certain sagacious foreigner has lately
used to striking effect, so that the chances between
Guido, doomed to death, and my aged self, were all in
favour of the doomed man outliving me, yet, were I
forthwith to appear before God and hear " Since by its
fruits a tree is judged, show me thy fruit, the latest
act of thine ! For in the last is summed the first and
all,—what thy life last put heart and soul into,
there shall I taste the product," I must plead this
condemnation of a man to-day. Not so ! At God's
Judgment bar there will be no questions, no answers,
no words, no juggling with speech ; none of the in-
eptitudes of words and arguments ; no coils of statement, no comment, query or response.
    He, the Truth, is, too, The Word. One truth
remains with us which we, whatever else as men we
question, still know irrefutably it is that I am I, as
He is He.   But, as I still am man, for me, while yet a
man, man's method, and so I appeal from myself as
Pope, to myself as man, my former self, my astute
worldly self, the self inquiring and dispassionate, and
before that self, e'er the burden of fourscore years and
six was laid upon me, I'll set Guido's case. This
younger self shall diligently question the after-me,
this self, now Pope.
    Now then I give my reasons why I find Guido a
guilty reprobate :—
    Guido had every advantage incident to a good start

in life. He had the ten talents, as it were. He had
one drawback, which he might have used as a stepping
stone, an incentive to good work. He was born into
a family that was not possessed of great riches, and so
neglecting all the great good things within his grasp
he hankered after those beyond the grating. This
greed and grasp of his, this convetousness, were beyond
most men's. He, this Guido, had such great gifts
as body and mind in balance, a sound frame, a solid
intellect, wit to seek, wisdom to choose, courage to
deal with circumstances, a great birth, traditionary
name, diligent culture, choice companionship and last,
but by no means least, conversancy with the faith, which
puts forth for its base of doctrine that man is not
born merely to content himself, but to please God,
became in fact three parts consecrate, that he might
be in a position to sue before the law for priest's
exemption where the layman sinned ; clothed himself
with the protection of the Church that he might violate
the law with impunity ! He, Guido, is nor more nor
less than that most irreligious of creatures a religious
parasite. His brothers are priests, and each felt
himself at liberty to do his murder in the Church's
pale,——
      I am reminded of that creature which I have seen
sometimes on the seashore, and which I have watched
by moonlight skulking along after its prey, having
detached itself from its shell and outside show. This
hermit crab, this naked slug thing, rid for the time of its
shell, fares ignobly with all loose and free, partaking
of the garbage feast of sandfly and slush-worm, a
naked blotch no better than they all. That's Guido !
Dropping his nobility and slipping the church, he
lays himself prostrate among the low vile things, and
then when Law catches him at his carrion prey he
points to the shell left high and dry and pleads " But
that's me ; the case out yonder." Nay but it *was*
thee Law found amid thine equals, congenial

vermin. That shell over there, that glory of pretence, that splendour with which thou hadst clothed thyself, that outside, was none of thee,—give it to the soldier-crab !

I see a special black mark, a mark that impinges Guido. It is that he believes in just the vile of life, and clothes himself in falsehood, scale on scale. He used the terms " honour " and " faith " merely as lies and disguise. Nor will I say that in this last Guido differs from other worldlings, for

> " All *say* good words
> To who will hear, all *do* thereby bad deeds
> To who must undergo ; so thrive mankind ! "

But now I will most carefully consider one of Guido's *latest* acts, and one moreover that touches the very core of his manhood. I sever this act from his life as sample ; show for Guido's self and test him by it. I speak of Guido's marriage. There's not a single motive I can find, of all the many that burst into act, that was a motive that should prompt him to it. There was not one permissible impulse ! He did not even like the maiden for her looks ; there was certainly no longing of a loving heart, not a trace of liking or of love ! His lust was not even such lust as the brutes know whose appetites are at least true. Guido feigned good motives, but his sole desire was gold. Lie, rob, if it must be, murder ! Make body and soul wring gold out ; use the name of love as a lure to draw the victim within the clutch of hate. Look, for a moment, with me at the picture in this man's mind, a picture he deliberately designed, and shaded, painting it according to the colours he selected. Here it is : The girl-wife, the old parents, were simply victims to be sacri-ficed to the greed of Guido. From Violante and Pietro were to be taken all the money, all the means that was theirs, and their hearts were to be wrung with anguish by the ill-treatment of their lamb-like innocent.

Insult and strenuous cruelty were to be applied to them until they should themselves seek to quit the roof which by the fraudulent promises made them, before they had parted with all they possessed was to be their "home." Then, when hunted forth to go hide head, starve and die, they would leave to him, Guido, the pale awe-stricken wife, past hope of help in the world now, mute and motionless, his slave, his chattel, to use and then destroy.

There's the picture, painted plain and Guido put all this in act and life, bending his mind to it, counting it the crown of earthly good to achieve success in it, and did not scruple to undertake, in God's face, a marriage, with all these lies so opposite God's truth, for ends so other than man's end. There's Guido's scheme ; that's the mind's picture, that picture shows the scheme he would have carried out, but he had over-looked the fact that even such sorry timid natures as those of the Comparini could lie and trick ! He found himself minutely matched—in the revelation of Pom-pilia's birth. He is piqued . . . and soars for a greater swoop in crime ;—he draws now on the curious crime, the fine felicity and flavour of wickedness, calling for the utmost exercise of crafty violence. To satiate his malice, and increase the pang of the parents, —he will torment their child yet within his reach. That's his move . . . watch him . . . he's not big enough for ordinary revenge . . . he chooses to sub-ordinate that to interest, the meaner sin ! He will torment his innocent wife that he may torture her parents, but he will not unclench his grasp and gripe of the money. So—day by day, hour by hour, he plagues her body and soul, that he may drive her to revolt,—to suicide—he hopes !—*This* will bring misery to the two old hearts that loved her ! This plan of his will ruin a trinity, if "successful," but leave him his luck, liberty, claims, "rights," person, and good fame unflawed, while they, on the contrary, will

lose everything—His cruelty will burn away their
happiness and make a ruin of their life and home.   He
will achieve this by the persistency of torment of the
girl-wife, so that in some awful moment, stung to
frenzy, she will break loose and fly anyhow, find refuge
anywhere,—it might be into the first arms opened
to save her from this monster, the arms of a pitiful
man.—

That dire moment came to the poor goaded child,
but the escape was not by way of sin.—O God, who
shall pluck sheep Thou holdest, from Thy hand?
Pompilia lay resigned to die—so far the cruelty was
foiled.—Again craft to supplement cruelty, and there is
simulated a love intrigue—false letters, false by every
test, not just the mere falseness of forged handwriting,
but false in spirit, as false as though the wretched
man had cut out shapes of filthy conceptions to paste
below the cherubs on a missal-page. See then, what
this Guido brings about and how far he is suffered to
proceed :—he is permitted to draw into a strange
temptation his wife, Pompilia, and the priest, Caponsacchi. These two are brought together as nor priest
nor wife should stand, and there is passion in the place,
power in the air for evil as for good, promptings from
heaven and hell, as if the stars fought in their courses
for a fate to be. Thus stand the wife and priest, a
spectacle, I doubt not, to unseen assemblage there.

> " No lamp will mark that window for a shrine,
> No tablet signalise the terrace, teach
> New generations which succeed the old,
> The pavement of the street is holy ground ;
> No bard describe in verse how CHRIST prevailed
> And Satan fell like lightning ! "

The second time Guido's plot fails, but this not by
counterplot, but by God's gift of a purity of soul that
will not take pollution, ermine-like armed from dishonour by its own soft snow. Such was this gift of

L

God, Who showed for once how He would have the world go white.

It seems to me as I pass all this in review, that a new *attribute* was born to both priest and wife,—a wonderful courage—-the courage of innocence. It sprang up to safeguard them, much as a thorn springs forward to defend the rose. Such a true courage, or courage of truth was it, that when it faced Guido, armed to his chattering teeth, he cowered and skulked behind law, which he called in to back his cowardice ! The law comes, hears, adjudicates and by its judgment gives Guido pause, to reflect. But what does Guido do ?

Do you see him stooping, peering, prying, prowling, muttering, as he looks about for that old broken trap of fraud, that indignant feet had kicked to ruin ? He discovers the fragments, picks them up, to the tiniest piece, and carries them to the old lurking place. Watch him trying to patch and refit the old things ; see him filing the blunt teeth anew, and setting it so that he may make sure next time that a snap shall break the bone. Craft, greed and violence complot revenge :——— Violence urges "Murder with jagged knife ! cut, but tear, too ! Foiled oft, starved long, glut malice for amends ! "—Once again Mercy holds out to Guido another chance . . . she brings him the olive branch . . . she seems to say "Sorrow is over accept ! " 'Tis an infant's birth, Guido's firstborn, his son and heir, that gives the occasion ; other men cut free their souls from care in such a case, fly up in thanks to God, reach, recognise His love for once : Guido cries " Soul, at last the mire is thine ! Lie there in likeness of a money-bag."

He sees in that son that any " rights " that he, Guido, may have in his wife are continued to him through their child, and that *now* he can, without endangering the gold, cut adrift the three lives he hates, one, the mother of his child ! Oh monster of a

man that can outrage thus both the woman and the
little child, and degrade fatherhood to that of the life
queller !——

Watch him yet, as intent on hellish devilry he
speaks a word, names a crime, appoints a price,
to four colourless-natured rustics. Suggests their
loyalty to him, and how he had suffered at the hands
of the Comparini three, and they, these country clowns,
who thought they had one virtue strong, loyalty to
the Franceschini, are suffused by him with his glowing
thought, red-hot from hell.

It is Christ's Birthnight-eve ! when we in Rome
would hear the angels' song, of " Peace on Earth
Goodwill to men," but that Christmas Eve brings to
our city the murderous five. Nine days pause again
had Guido ! Nine days was his hand held back. Then
was the murder managed and sin thereby conceived
to the full : and why not crowned with triumph too ?
Why ?—God's touch o' the tether . . . a check . . .
did Guido—guess—why ? Pulled up Guido ! A slight
touch on the rein ! Ha ! Guido. Who gave you
memory, Guido ? How came it that that memory
failed in one small particular ? Forgetfulness of what
you best know ! Every urchin knows that to leave
Rome to get horses, you must show the warrant, the
ordinary clerk's scribble. . . . How many times,
Guido, you the resident in Rome for thirty years have
so instructed strangers ? And now, just at this crucial
moment, when to you it is a matter of life and death,
you find that your memory has " failed " you . . .
or is it, Guido, that God has remembered ?——

So, tired and footsore, those blood-flustered five
went reeling on the road through dark and cold a few
miles, then sank down to sleep in the first wayside
straw, . . . and so were caught and caged ! You say
it was all through one little trip, a trick of Memory,
a touch of the fool in the astute Guido ? He curses the
omission more than the murder ! He sees not, blind

fool that he is, that *that* was just God's mercy-stroke that stopped his fate. His comrades in murder had all made up their minds to slay him ? Why ? He had the money with him which he had promised them as the price of blood, but the deed done he refused to pay them, and they, indignant at this breach of faith, had made up their minds to get rid of him and seize that to which they considered that they were entitled.

Such I, the Pope, and the man who once was *not* the Pope, find Guido, the midmost blotch of black in all that Franceschini group. The master's hand is that of this fox-faced horrible Abate Paolo, Guido's brother ! Why mere wolfishness looks well, and Guido himself honest in the red o' the flame, beside this yellow that would pass for white. . . . While Guido brings the struggle to a close, Paul steps back the due distance, clear o' the trap he builds and baits. Paul's case is reserved for judgment, it will not be given in my time. Then there's that hybrid, Girolamo, the younger brother. I see a new distinctive touch in him—lust ! hell's own blue tint, that gives a character and marks the man more than a match for yellow and red. Then comes the hag that gave these three abortions birth, unmotherly mother and unwomanly woman that near turns motherhood to shame.

The last I see as partners in this crime are scarcely more than boys, in years none exceeding twenty ! They come from the country too, not from the crowded city ! What would one expect to hear from them when invited to such crime ? Surely an indignant outcry against such work ! but no ! no more demur than if they had been asked to dig a vineyard ! Was it their old fond faith in the lord of the land ? Nothing of the kind it was all done purely for pay ! This is attested by how they turned on him and would have killed him and rifled the gold.

I recall the only answer of the Governor, to whom

the defenceless Pompilia appealed, a threat and a shrug of the shoulder.

I save my little word for the Archbishop, who is under me, as I am under God :—didst thou not turn and flee as a mere hireling when the little lamb, pressed hard by the wolf, panted at thy feet. . . . I've a sure word for thee, Archbishop !

It is time the light flooded the dark cave of iniquity and purified the scene.

But I turn from the contemplation of hell to hell's despair, as I see it in that beam of beauty, Pompilia. First of the first, such I pronounce her, then as now perfect in whiteness. All the intellect of man, his energy and his knowledge look to me small, poor, beside the marvel of such a soul as Pompilia holds up, as earth's flower, to the face of God ! Poor, humble little girl ! It was not given her to know much, speak much, or write a book to move mankind—yet if in purity and patience, if in faith held fast despite the plucking fiend . . . if in right returned for wrong, most pardon for worst injury . . . then will this woman-child have proved . . . just the one prize vouchsafed unworthy me.

See there my garden! For ten years I tended it; not carelessly and with slack hand, but with sweat and blood I've tilled the untoward ground. All day, that long ten years I worked, and now at dusk there's at least one blossom that makes me proud at eventide, and it sprang forth mid the briers of my enclosure. Once again I see the nothingness of man ! Those plants to which I specially looked for blossom, keeping them under the master's eye, as it were, they gave such poor results, such timid leaves, such uncertain flowers —but this mere chance-sown cleft-nursed seed, that sprang up by the wayside, neath the foot of the enemy, this breaks into a blaze of glory, from the inch height whence it looks and longs.

My flower, my rose, I gather for the breast of God,

I find this best in thee, where all was yet so good, that having endured all, when it but concerned thyself, didst cease to despise thine own life when the first low word of God fell on thy fine ear attuned, " Value life and preserve life for My sake." Thy spirit did mingle with that of universal motherhood to worthily defend that trust of trusts, Life from the Ever Living. Thou didst accept the obligation laid on thee, mother elect, to save the unborn child, hesitating not to draw the sword in such defence !

> " Go past me
> And get thy praise,—and be not far to seek
> Presently when I follow if I may ! "

Now I turn me a little from Pompilia, to my warrior-priest, Caponsacchi.   Maybe in thee I see the rose of gold, graven to imitate God's miracle—I shall not put thee so very far away from her ! It is true that in the accompaniments of thine action I find much amiss —this freak of thine.   I might criticise the masquerade, the change of garb, but I praise and admire that which was grandly done, the athlete's leap amongst the uncaged beasts, set upon the martyr-maid in the uncaged cirque.   In his impulsive promptitude he championed God at first blush, answering the challenge of the false knight ringingly.   But,—here is a sad question—Where were the *Church's men-at-arms*, while this man, in mask and motley has to do their work ?   What did he do besides pray ' Lead us not in temptation ? '   When it came he met it like a man, mastered it, made it crouch beneath his feet, seized it by the head and hair and did battle with it, while those of the Church who had been specially drilled to take their part in standing for the right, failed to respond to the real cry, this man, whose swordhand was used to strike the lute, pushed forward, shamed the laggards and retrieved the day.   Well done !   Be glad thou hast let light into the world, through that

irregular breach of the boundary. Notwithstanding
he must ruminate, once more work, be unhappy but
bear life !

Now I turn my mind toward God ; I reach into the
dark, and feel what I cannot see. I review the order
of the Universe. I collect my thoughts and see man's
mind as a convex glass wherein are gathered all the
scattered points picked out of the immensity of sky,
and reuniting them, and revealing God to man ! Angel
and insect, each to capacity is full of God, showing,
as it were, a facet of love. This tale supplies the
one instance needed of *love without limit* ; unlimited
in self-sacrifice. I view God this way and I see Him
complete. I can believe that man's life on earth has
been devised that he may wring from all his pain the
pleasures of eternity. I see this life as a training, a
preparation, a passage ; and even Guido, in that other
world, that life beyond death, may run the race and
win the prize.

> " We are not babes, but know the minute's worth,
> And feel that life is large and the world small,
> So, wait till life have passed from out the world."

Let me ask myself am I astonished that whereas I
can receive and trust God's plan, other men,
made with hearts and souls the same as mine, reject
and disbelieve,—subordinate the future to the present,
—sin, nor fear ? No ! It is not *that* that astonishes
me. It is rather that those who have once found the
pearl of faith, should then turn, and with double zest
go and dredge for whelks, mud-worms that make the
savoury soup. These are worldlings !

But now, I turn me to look how the Christians deport
themselves ! What do I find ? The Archbishop, at
whose feet she threw herself, to whom she cried,
" Protect me from the fiend," tosses her back to the
fiend, to keep him quiet. It was failure, too, with
the friar, who was supposed to have forsaken the world,

and to be disregardless of its praise or blame. What
did he ? Shrank from interfering where his betters
held back, for fear of blame, and so broke his promise
leaving her to break her heart. Thus do these Christians battle for the faith ! Well they were individuals,
and weak, standing alone. What shall I find if I look
at many weak individuals banded together for strength,
in the Monastery called " Convertites," meant to
help women because these helped Christ. The very
idea of the existence of this Convent is *action*. Pompilia is sent to these for help. They are quick to
testify to her pure life and saintly, dying days. She
dies and lo, who seemed so poor, proves rich. Now
what does the body of women-to-help-women do ?
They unsay all the fine speeches, and try to prove her a
woman of loose life for, if they can succeed in their
proof, her property comes to them !

Why, as I see it, the wrangling of the Roman soldiers,
as they threw dice, for the coat of Christ, was a small
offence to the greed of the apostles, disputing, as it
were, whether the garment were, after all, His !
Is this the best fruit I can take with me to show
as a result of my stewardship ? When I contrast how
Caponsacchi sprang forward to help at the cry " For
Pity's sake," with the way that the panoplied Christians slunk into corners, I am terrified ! Oh, I hear
the hubbub of protestation from monks and friars,
who begin to recite all that down the ages they have
done. My answer is that for all that you have done as
Christians, I can show you another doughtiness to
match, done at the instinct of the natural man. Where
is the immeasurable metamorphosis of human clay
to divine gold that was to be the outcome of the Cross ?
Why, if an adept in gold-work obtained no better
results than an ordinary rule-of-thumb worker, what
should we say ? So, when that Great Power who made
man body and soul, ordained salvation for them both
and yet . . . well, is the thing we see, salvation ?

I have but one answer to this question, and it suffices
me. " The light that did burn will burn ! " . . . I
never miss my footing in the maze, no, I have light nor
fear the dark at all.

But are mankind not real, who pace outside the petty
circle the world measured me ? Are they merely phan-
toms, ghosts ? Their cry is other. Out of the old times
have stepped forth philosophers and bards and boldly
proclaimed the truth. They taught " The inward
work and worth of any mind what other mind may
judge save God, who only knows the thing He made,
the veritable service He exacts ? " If Euripides
should ask me the question " Pope, dost thou dare
pretend to punish me, for not descrying sunshine at
midnight, . . . (two thousand years back, long before
the Christ had dwelt here) while thou rewardest teachers
of the truth, who miss the plain way in the blaze of
noon—(why even a word of my teaching if strongly
applied had saved them wallowing in that mire of
cowardice and slush of lies)." What answer should I
give Euripides ? There's a legend to the effect that
Paul answered Seneca, but that was in the day-
spring ; noon is now, we have got too familiar with the
light. The torpor of assurance has become such that
the spirit of the martyrs that gladly gave their bodies
to hasten, as they believed, the day of Christ's coming
to make all things new, has died down and faded out.
There is no recognition of the significance of pain,—
from glory of pain to glory of joy—such as they
knew, when they gladly relinquished all things earthly,
even earthly loves, to find them again later, and finite
love blent and embalmed with its eternal life. What
whispers come to me from the Future age ? I hear them
tell, of the approaching times, that in them the torpor
of assurance shall be shaken ; discarded doubts will
be reintroduced ; old reports will be discredited and
the towers of faith shall be shaken by earthquake.
Then . . . then . . . multitudes will sink from the

plane of Christianity, down, down to the next stopping
place, the next base, the lust and the pride of life !

" Surely some one Pompilia in the world
Will say ' I know the right place by foot's feel,
I took it and tread firm there ; wherefore change ? "

but the multitude, the mass of men, whose very souls
even now seem to need re-creating,—so they slink
worm-like into the mud light now lays bare,—these,
though baptised and grafted into Christ lie as dead.
Those who with all the aid of Christ lie thus, how much
deeper, without Christ, would they sink ?—Capon-
sacchis by their mere impulse will be guided right ;
the majority will obey instincts which are diverse to
right.   There will be men of the same type of mind as
the Abate Paolo—men who like the lowest of life's
appetites, and live for greed, ambition, lust, revenge ;
yet other leaders will be like Guido, who will beckon
low intelligences to do any dirty work that they require
done, offering to reward them with money.
    Still I stand here on life's stage, armed by God not
only with Peter's key, but with Paul's sword ! I
gather to me all my strength and smite, so ending this
offence.   Just as my arm is raised to strike, my sleeve
is plucked by whom ? O, they are " friends," of course,
who are sorry I am inclined to strike so roughly ;
they plead " spare him " (Guido) and urge that by
signing his death warrant I shall send him out of life
with his sin full on him ! Remonstrance on all sides
begins instruct me, there's a new tribunal now, higher
than God's—the educated man's ! Here are arguments set out, filling a hundred lines, and giving a
score of reasons why I should put back my sword.
What says the Advocate here ? " The pardon, Holy
Father ! . . . Our tears on tremble, hearts big with a
benediction, wait the word shall circulate through the
city in a trice, set every window flaring, give each

man o' the mob his torch to waive for gratitude."
They urge me to pronounce the word !

> " I will, Sirs : for a voice other than yours
> Quickens my spirit : I write, God guiding my hand :
> ' On receipt of this command
> Acquaint Count Guido and his fellows four
> They die to-morrow ; could it be to-night,
> The better, but the work to do takes time.
> Set with all diligence a scaffold up,
> Not in the customary place, by Bridge
> Saint Angelo, where die the common sort ;
> But, since the man is noble, and his peers
> By predilection haunt the People's Square,
> There let him be beheaded in the midst,
> And his companions hanged on either side :
> So shall the quality see, fear and learn.
> All which work takes time : till to-morrow, then,
> Let there be prayer incessant for the five ! ' "

And then what ?

For Guido I've no hope except in such a suddenness
of fate that the truth, like a lightning flash, may
reveal to him a sight that shall be salvation. Just
as the vivid lightning parts the dark and shows the
hid city, so may this sudden blow on Guido provide
the flash by which he shall see, one instant, and be
saved. . . .

Enough, for I may die this very night, and how
should I dare die, this man let live ?

Carry this forthwith to the Governor !

BOOK No. XI

GUIDO

BOOK No. XI

" GUIDO "

My Dear Friend,

That week I spent as the dying Pompilia was sad, but infinitely sadder is the week I am spending as the condemned Guido. It is not the fact of the condemnation, it is not the prison-cell, nor the fact that it is a dark, filthy place, nor yet the old friends come to minister in this hour, but it is that I, Guido Franceschini, have been placed in such a desperate position ! The absurd over-sight, trick of memory, which deprived me of escape—faugh ! The devil's in it ! On the stone bench in this fetid cell, with the vapour of an agony drawn of perpetual thwartings of as perpetual schemings, struck into drops on the cold wall and crawling worm-like down, I sit and am racked in mind. Yes, there's a lamp ; not on my account is it there but for the two,—Cardinal and Abate—in old days my friends, who have come to minister to me ! Well *I'll* speak and they shall hear . . . they shall hear such words as they'll never succeed in wiping out of memory. I'll speak plainly : I've done with honeyed phrases . . . I'll give the tiger in me liberty.

To the Cardinal : " So you are the Cardinal Acciaiuoli and *you* (to the Abate) are Abate Panciatichi— two good Tuscan names ! It was your ancestor, Cardinal, that erected that huge block of buildings over the little Greve, the rivulet that turns at the foot of the hill just as Florence comes into sight. That other little rivulet, Ema . . . I remember, was a place loved by the kingfishers which flocked to the Ema bridge. . . . I do adjure you help me Sirs ! My blood comes from as

fine a source, from as far back, as yours—It should not
be allowed to leak through scaffold planks into Rome's
sink where her red refuse runs !

This is a trick, your coming here at break of day.
A trick to startle me into further truth-telling ! Pshaw !
It would take more than that kind of play to fright a
Franceschini. Feel my pulse ; its steady, isn't it ?
I'm innocent—as innocent as babe, as Mary mother, as
innocent as Pope Innocent (my murderer !). I said it,
say and repeat it.—Only twelve hours ago the gaoler
looked in and bade me get a good sleep and wake up a
free man, and now you tell me to prepare for death twelve
hours hence ! Its monstrous ! Rome, the manly part
of Rome, knows well that I struck out a good blow
for it. . . . Each man who was honest and owned
wife, sister, daughter, mistress, would feel outraged
were I to suffer this accursed death ! My knavish
lawyers held that *if* all else failed I still had one plea
at least would hold—the Clergy's plea.

The Pope, old Innocent, meek, mild, merciful, fond
of the poor, a very angel in man's likeness,—he was to
help us at a pinch,—but when we are at grip with death,
what does he do, fifty thousand devils in deepest hell !
but send us death—! Does he think for a single moment
that my death will do his memory credit ?

" But law ! "—Well, what of that ? Law lays before
him the very chance to save my life. Law has dropped
into his open palm my life ! What does he do with it ?
Sighs, shakes his head and refuses to shut his hand on
it ! Nay even motions away the gift my lawyers bade
him grasp. Disinterested Vicar of our Lord. He
offers me as a sop to the 'good and right'.

Sir Abate, *can you do nothing* ? Remember when we
were boys together ! All the break-neck escapades we
indulged ; all the pleasant byeways we took, as did our
forbears—why I can show you just the spot where my
grandfather stabbed a knave for a mere gibe . . . and
now—now, why look at my plight because I played a

prank my grandsire played,—and with my very good
reason too ! Here I lie sprawling in a trap set by the
" good " old Pope. I'm to be used as a warning !
I'm to illustrate law ! I'm to be sacrificed for the glory
of the Pope and the good of my fellows !

He has sent you two here to announce that in twelve
hours he'll try upon my body and soul a brand new
engine for repressing pranks. Do you know what that
engine's like ? Do you feel already its sharp teeth biting
into soft throat ? . . . No ! what you fine friends are
thinking is that to-night, at suppertime, you'll entertain the company with talk of Guido's last hours, last
sayings. . . . I see the guests jump up to welcome his
Eminence who shrived the wretch ! . . . Then they
all reseat, and compose themselves to listen to the
Abate's story !

Think, Sirs, of all the white haired, shrunken
shrivelled up old people who will be alive, when my
full-blooded body will lie lifeless ! Is it not terrible, I
entreat you Sirs ? Is it not terrible I say to be so much
alive and yet—to die— ? Now I see all my life—honey
yet gall of it . . . there my life's lying—now, now I see,
feel, hear, know *all* of it . . . but death. . . . Oh Sirs,
be pitiful . . . save me !

Do you see my folly, in my wife ? I was a fool to
believe the absurd saw that a man requires a woman and
a wife. I knew that just myself concerned myself.
Why wasn't I content with that knowledge ? Why the
woman's in the man ! . . . Why all that unmanly
appetite for truth, careless courage as to consequence,
intuition, burning words, these were never mine . . .
They are Pompilia's . . . the woman-side of me,
turned foremost. But I was going to tell you . . .
the man in me . . . of the Pope's " new engine "
Mannaia. I've seen it ; the hateful thing ! I saw the
thing . . . had it explained to me, when it came down
on the head of Felice What's-his-name who had dared
to strike the Duke to slap him in the face for kidnapping

M

a girl, a sister of Felice, who sat and sang, while she
plaited fringe, in the filthy doorway. The narrow
beams, the iron plate with the sharp shearing edge, the
half moon collar, the other half,—which two halves
encircle the neck— . . . I feel the blade drop on
me . . . whiz . . . down drops the head . . . cut
trundles body . . . *where's your soul gone ?* That too
I shall find ! . . . That evening the Duke gave a
reception, was congratulated by his friends that Felice
had lost his head ! He bowed, smiled and handed
round a portrait, painted, of the sister, as Europa on
the back o' the bull. " Better that than virginity in
rags," were his words, and everybody laughed. There
was a Pope alive then, just as much as now ! But he's
quite another Pope . . . and I, Guido Franceschini
do the Duke's deed but take Felice's place ! I lose my
head ! Pretty term to apply to a head ! Lose a ker-
chief or a snuff box or a bauble and you can replace it ;
lose a limb and you can make wood take its place,
but Lord ! a wooden head . . . ! I know how a head
is set on. Didn't my fencing-master teach me how to
guard mine and thrust the anatomy of my opponents ?
But fencing is an art. The Pope's engine is a thing of
brute force, cutting as it comes ; it breaks in, breaks out
o' the hard and soft of you—ugh— !
        And why, why must this be ? Oh if men were but
good ! They are not good, nowise like Peter : people
called him rough. . . . I could have petitioned him
and he would surely answer " Free him and forgive his
fault." The Pope is in Peter's place, surely it's his
bounden duty to forgive ! Oh Pope Innocent you
profess yourself tender for souls—Christ's maxim is
—one soul outweighs the world—therefore respite me,
save a soul, curse the world ! What is the answer ?
The secular power has entrusted the final finding to the
spiritual—the fitting compliment by way of answer is
that the spiritual shall out do the mere legal in harsh-
ness. Don't stand there you two putting on that

professional face . . . you know perfectly well that I've
summed up your answer ; see through your casuistry.
Dear my friends do but see ! Just because I've had
the best o' the battle in defending myself the Pope who
as a good shepherd of the flock should help the helpless
sheep by hooking the creature into safety with his
guiding crook, reverses it instead and thrusts with
point the shuddering sheep he calls a wolf back and
down and down to where hell gapes. . . . What's
that you advise me ? Repent ! What good will that
do me ? Suppose I spent the next twelve hours repent-
ing—would that fact assist the engine halfway back
into its hiding house ? Ah, but that is not quite your
meaning ! You offer me a chance of saving my soul in
the minute betwixt this world and the next. Well
truth shall save it since no lies will help. Now then
Civilisation and Society prepare to hear the truth. I
must make up my mind to death you say ! It is just
in the way that I cry for respite that that old Pietro
cried, when I chased him here and there, morsel by
morsel cut away the life I loathed. Time to confess,
he asked, nay entreated. Much respite did I grant !
Why grant me respite who deserve my doom ? I
recognise that in the old times when things began a
sort of pact was made for the good of all that none should
take their pleasure by others' pain. Law was set to
watch, and decided that things which give too much
pleasure to individuals are wicked and occasion the
reprisal of the envious ! Law enjoins punishment for
those who seize their neighbours' share. Well, I
infringed law. I broke bond, and needs must pay
price—wherefore here's my head flung with a flourish !
That's not enough that I pay the price but you ask me
for repentance too ! My repentance is that I ineptly
blundered, not that I broke any law ! You Cardinal
and Abate know perfectly well that belief is one thing,
profession another. That the works wrought by belief
might just as easily and well be wrought by unbelief. ..

What, you try to stop my mouth with the Crucifix !
Off with it. Look in your own heart, if your soul
have eyes ! Do you, either of you, suppose that I
don't understand why you crook or cringe, fast or
feast, praise, blame, sit, stand, lie or go ! Suppose
one of the Pope's halberdiers, standing on sentry
duty were suddenly to fling down his halbert and rush
into the Pope's presence, instantly aware and over-
whelmingly convinced of sin. The Pope, maybe, is
talking to the Ambassador, but he leaves him and bids
him wait while he gains a soul, said to be worth
the whole world ! Just so that same sentry, if he knew
that a powder mine were beneath the Pope's feet might
rush into the presence, to save the mere body of the
Pope ! Why, come to that a man would act as quickly
to save a jewel case, or at any rate its contents, and
yet . . . yet my life, you, my boon companions, men
who took part with me in all buffoonery, now declare
is forfeit, for the general good, and will not interpose
or enter the Pope's presence and plead for me. You
will do nothing, but are content just to advise me
prepare for death ! But each minute as I talk this
Mannaia-machine draws an inch nearer me. Fool,
Fool !

> You understand me and forgive, sweet Sirs ?
> I blame you, tear my hair and tell my woe—
> All's but a flourish, figure of rhetoric !
> One must try each expedient to save life.

At least admit that my defence is plausible, and that's
the utmost that can be said in favour of the best belief
held.

> " Saint Somebody-or-other raised the dead."
> " Did he ? How do you come to know as much ? "
> " Know it, what need ? The story's plausible,
>   Avouched for by a martyrologist."

In the same way can't you see that even if I were
mistaken in the story of my wife's infidelity, yet that

I believed it, to me it was plausible. Though to all
the world it might have seemed that my wife was a
true wife and pure, that the priest was true and that
old pair of liars, Pietro and Violante, true, yet, concede, that they might seem false to just one man in the
world, and that man maddened by jealousy ! Just
as the sting of a thousand gnats—each gnat a tiny
creature in itself, might induce pain as great as serpent's
sting, so the many sly soft stimulants to wrath at last
induced in me that outburst that gave general revenge.
Then you come along and take each tiny individual
wrong and accuse me of an *excessive* crime !

Jealousy ! What has it not caused in the way of
crime ? The playwrights, painters sculptors, artists in
general, have pointed their Art depicting its effects.
But the moment I, a jealous husband, step forth . . .
why, instead of an understanding admiration, what do
you offer me— ?   I'm expected to look through that
stoniest of stone walls, the heart, and see it through and
through ! Such an eye God's may be,—not yours or
mine.   But I'm talking again ! What is the time ?

> Away with man ! What shall I say to God ?
> This, if I find the tongue and keep the mind—
> " Do Thou wipe out the being of me, and smear
> This soul from off the white of things, I blot !
> I am one huge and sheer mistake,—whose fault ?
> Not mine at least, who did not make myself ! "
> Someone declares my wife excused me so !
> Perhaps she knew what argument to use.
> Grind your teeth Cardinal, Abate, writhe !
> What else am I to cry out in my rage,
> Unable to repent one particle o' the past ?

You both persist, in your shallow judgment and want
of sense, in calling my blunder a *crime* !   At the worst
I stood in doubt at the cross-roads and took one path
of many.   Oh we all see *now* exactly where that path
led, but nobody saw, at first, that it ended in the red !

Now suppose you had both been by to advise me when
I took the first false step—well what would you have
said, " Love your wife " ?   There she stands, the alive
pale thirteen year old, milk-for-blood, child Pompilia.
I can see that little room at Via Vittoria, the mother's
arm round the girl's waist, to hold her back from her
playthings, which as I entered she had left, scared at my
appearance, wondering that I could look so grim.   She
is struck dumb by sight of me ; she is repelled by me.
She clearly shows that she would bear any cross rather
than be with me.   You are touched with pity ? I
am touched but to resentment.   We only show man's
soul through man's flesh, she sees mine, it strikes her
thus !—Therefore 'tis she begins with wronging me,
who cannot but begin with hating her.   Our marriage
follows : there we stand again ! I laugh now, even in
the face of death, as I think of it ! This spark of mirth
at this time may be a hellish toy, but there it is ! We
stand in the Church, lovers,—waiting the ceremony.
She, Pompilia, is just an automaton.   When the mother
speaks the word she obeys it, as though by so speaking
the mother had wound up a mechanical toy and set it
thereby to certain movements.   What you call my
wife I call a nullity in female shape, vapid disgust,
soon to be pungent plague, and that to be made more
pungent yet by the cunning smug mother, and the
idiotic tom-fool father.   You blame me that I was
angry ? How could I be otherwise ? I fooled the old
pair that meant to fool me ; they first insult me, I
return the blow, there follows noise enough—hue and
cry, whimpering and wail, a perfect goose-yard cackle
of complaints.   I opened the door and swept them out,
bade them go whine elsewhere.   I was just rejoicing
in the silence when my goose and gander clapped wing
and crew, fighting-cock fashion,—they had filched a
pearl from dungheap and might boast with cause
enough ! I was defrauded of all bargained for,—you
know, the Pope knows, not a soul but knows—

My dowry was derision, my gain—muck,
My wife (the Church declared my flesh and blood)
The nameless bastard of a common whore :
My old name turned henceforth to . . . shall I say
" He that received the ordure in his face ? "

And they, my wrongers, actually rounded myself in the
ears with my own wrong, themselves secure under the
mantle of the believing public cast over them that they
were " too stupid to invent " too simple to distinguish
wrong from right—while I was the violent oppressor
whom heaven would punish by them ! But, you urge,
Pompilia, she was free of guile, unimplicate in crime.
. . . I'll go back to the time when she was left alone
with me at Arezzo. I say to her " Pompilia, who
declare that you love God, remember that God said
' Thy desire shall be to thy husband,' then I, your
husband say, desire my love, yield me contentment and
be ruled aright ! " She sits up, she lies down, she
comes and goes, kneels at the couch side, overleans the
sill o' the window, cold and pale and mute as stone,
strong as stone also. I say to her " Well, are they not
fled ? Am not I left, am I not one for all ? Speak a
word, drop a tear, detach a glance, bless me or curse me
of your own accord ! Is it the ceiling only wants your
soul ? " She brings her eyes down and looks at me.
" Speak," I say ; she obeys, " Be silent ! " she obeys,
counting the minutes till I cry " Depart " as brood-
bird when you saunter past her eggs departed, just
the same through door and wall, I see the same
stone strength of white despair. And all this will never
be otherwise ! Her worst offence of all was not offend-
ing more, but just giving up the game. She wound up
her beautiful long black hair into a mere wisp, made her
dress trim and neat, gave up springing out of bed when
I got in, and imploring me to leave her free,—I might
have wrung her neck,—she'd have said nothing—
merely sighed and shown a moment's disquiet in her
eyes. Had I bade her cut off her hair, she'd have taken

scissors and have laid a yard or so on the floor. She
sits still and stares !

Let none think to bear that look of steady wrong,
endured as steadily. . . . This self-possession to the
uttermost, how does it differ in aught, save degree,
from the terrible patience of God ?   " All which just
means she did not love you ! " you say. That was no
reason why she shouldn't *show* love . . . love the sham
does twice the service done by love, the true. . . . All
women cannot give men love, forsooth ! no nor all
pullets lay the henwife eggs—the chalk ball in the nest
starts them. . . . My wife was of another mood—
she would not begin the lie that ends with truth, nor
feign the love that brings real love about ; wherefore
I judged, sentenced and punished her. What's that
you say I ought to have left the adventure of marriage
untried ? . . . . Ay my friend, easy to say, easy to
do ; step right now you've stepped left and stumbled
on—the red thing. Do you think that I doubt any
more than you that practice makes perfect ? I, by
this time, am so practised, that I've grown fit guide for
myself. . . . Ah well, time's running out ! All I
mean to say by all this is that my wife proved a true
stumbling block in the way of me, her husband. . . .
I but plied the hatchet you yourselves use to clear
a path. . . .   there'd have been a very different judgment had things gone well at the wayside inn. Think
how the world would have applauded had I found the
runaways asleep together at the inn and run my sword
through them ! The fact is in all this my luck was
against me. My way with the woman, now proved
grossly wrong, just missed of being gravely, grandly
right ! When I took the assassins to the Villa I was
fortunate in finding all at home—the three to kill ;
but my luck turned when I endeavoured to escape.
Again, I with my knowledge of anatomy thought that
I had surely killed my wife, but she lingered on for four
days, the doctor keeping life in her body as long as he

could that all Rome might listen to her story.   If she
had not told it I would have told mine ; I would have
sworn that I caught Pompilia in Caponsacchi's arms,
and that he had escaped in the darkness.   But just
see the irony of it all, she has lived to " forgive " me,
to " commend me to the mercies of God," at the same
time fixing my head on the block.   See again my ill
luck evidenced in the trial.   Why try to play a game
with hopes of winning, when the dice are loaded against
one ?   Yet I know . . . I am certain that the people
of Rome approve my deed, while actually the mob is in
love with my murdered wife !   Well, this I will say, she
knew not how to hate ;   there wasn't a touch of it in
her.   The angels of the heaven above would have an
impossible task to make a heaven for her if she knew
that I were in hell, why she'd pray me into heaven
against my will !—Yes, against my will, so heartily do
I hate the good. . . . I demand hell, as a right—You
see, you hear ;   there's no spark of contrition in me.
Is then the Church satisfied to slay the impenitent ? . . .
   Cardinal take away your crucifix ! Abate, leave my
lips alone,—they bite ! I have bared my heart . . .
you bathe it, but it grows the stonier for your saving
dew ! . . . Rave another twelve hours, every word
were waste ! Cardinal, you know I am wronged !
Wronged, say, and wronged maintain.   When you
were first made a Cardinal there was no such strict
inquisition for blood ! . . . Why your very way lay
across others—brained heads, broken hearts,—lives
trodden into dust. . . . Does memory haunt your
pillow ? You can't even take an innocent walk in your
garden without treading out the life of a universe of
happy innocent things ! A fly buzzes near your mouth
and flaps your face.   You blot it from being at a blow.
It was a fly you were a man, and Lord of created things.
. . . Just so I took my course and why, therefore,
must the Pope kill me ? . . . The Pope who dooms me
needs must die next year ;—shall I tell you the chances

for his successor ? . . . You stand seventh on the list,
. . . unless . . . . ha, ha, How can a dead hand give
a friend a lift ? . . . Cardinal, I adjure you in God's
name, save my life, fall at the Pope's feet set forth
things your own fashion . . . " Count Guido must not
die, is innocent . . . but if he were blood-drenched
from head to foot, yet spare him whose death insults
the Emperor. . . . He has friends who will avenge him,
enemies who will hate God now with impunity . . . .
would you send a soul straight to perdition ? He is
now a frank atheist." Go and say this for God's
sake !

You don't think that I even hope you'll say one single
word in my behalf, surely ? I know you better, Cardinal.—Take your crucifix away, I tell you, for the
second time ! The Pope's dead now, my murderous old
man, for Tozzi told me so : as for you, Abate, that
hacking cough of yours will carry you off in less than
a year. . . . Go eat your heart out Cardinal, you'll
never be Pope. . . . Tell me, is it true that you deserted
your affianced bride, who is since dead, for promotion
in the Church. . . . You'll all follow me soon, pushing
me to the front, as I go first, and reach a minute sooner
than was meant the boundary whereon I break to
mist. . . . You never know what life means till you
die ; death gives the spice to life ; death makes the
significance of love and faith. . . . On earth I never
took the Pope for God, in heaven I shall scarce take
God for the Pope.

> All that was, is : and must forever be,
> Nor is it in me to unhate my hates,—
> I use up my last strength to strike once more

Old Pietro, beast Violante, and I grow one gorge to
loathingly reject Pompilia's pale poison my hasty
hunger took for food. . . . I lived and died a man,
and take man's chance, honest and bold : right will
be done to such.

Who are these you have let descend my stair ?
Ha, their accursed psalm ! Lights at the sill !
Is it " Open " they dare bid you ? Treachery !
Sirs, have I spoken one word all this while
Out of the world of words I had to say ?
Not one word ! All was folly,—I laughed and mocked !
Sirs, *my first true word* all truth and no lie,
Is—save me notwithstanding ! Life is all !˙
I was just stark mad,—let the madman live
Pressed by as many chains as you please pile !
Don't open ! Hold me from them ! I am yours,
I am the Granduke's—no, I am the Pope's !
Abate,—Cardinal,—Christ,—Maria,—God, . . .
POMPILIA, will you let them murder me ?

BOOK No. XII

" THE BOOK AND THE RING "

BOOK No. XII

MY DEAR FRIEND,

Here were the end, had anything an end, but even the rocket that goes up with a roar, and a soar, and a rush comes down like a stick, and then all that is left is a memory of a brilliance that has been . . . that was . . . maybe the darkness is blacker because of the past light.

Glaring Guido, ghastly Guido ; a flash and all that was left of the glare was a something, two somethings, a head and a trunk, but the separation even if they two could have been joined again would not have made Guido ! All that is left of him here is a *memory*, of what ? That depends on the remembrancer !

Here am I, Robert Browning, once again myself, after having been so many minds in one, I now, freeing my own Ego from the crowd of Egos that have possessed me, by turns—nor yet always waiting turn, but frequently together—I Robert Browning, poet and student of men and women, look about me again, in this year 1868,—one hundred and seventy years since that day when Guido and his hirelings were found of death, and I find, concerning that day, four letters yet extant, and but four. I will take them as they come. The first is from a stranger, a man of rank, a Venetian visitor, at Rome. He is writing on the evening of *the* day. He says : " The Carnival is at an end : crowds of people are here yet, strangers from all parts who will jostle each other for a good place when that befalls fate cannot long defer. The Pope is old, and totters on the verge of the grave. I don't believe much in his doctor . . . he's not equal to the other, Malpichi, but even the best doctor could do

but little for him on account of his great age.   A week
ago he took exercise in the warm May sunshine beside
the river ; he loved to see that Custom-house he built
upon the bank, for being Naples-born his love for the
sea is easily understood.   He has frequent fainting fits,
or else he lies in stupor.   His heart is still set on lasting
till December next that he may hold Jubilee a second
time and, for a second time, also, open the Holy Doors.

By the by tell Dandolo I've lost my wager and owe
him fifty gold zecchines : The Pope has done his worst
and I have to pay for the execution of the Count—
by Jove !

Only two days ago I believed with all Rome that he
was safe, and reported so, little suspecting the deaf ear
of the Pope.   I had no idea that his prejudicies were
so strong ! But they fairly got the better in the man.

As he walks about he lets the crowd question him
and it is said that they asked him whether murder was
a privilege only reserved for nobles like the Count,—
and he, this Pope, was ever mindful of the mob !
Martiniez, who pleaded hard and long for Guido's life,
urging that he might well be one with whom he had
dined, will not soon forgive the Pope's rebuff . . . he
could hardly be persuaded to attend the execution
. . . wouldn't have come if it hadn't been for a lady
who interests him, as it was he'd scarcely cast a glance
at the spectacle from where he sat.   Staging was
erected in the Place, and windows of the Three Streets
were let at six dollars each :—

Directly the Pope's decision was made known,
Acciaoli and Panciatichi, old friends and compatriots
of the condemned Count, were chosen to acquaint
Guido with the finding, and they stayed with him all
night, until dawn, and they both report that their last
efforts to compose the mind of the nobleman for a good
ending were successful.   At 2 p.m. the Company of
Death arrived and the Count was led down, hoisted
up on car, the last of the five, being the worst culprit,

you know. Everybody saw his nonchalance ! Everybody admired it ! The procession started and took the way from the New Prisons to the Place o' the People, where " Mannaia " stands. Its a long route—by Pilgrim's Street, Governo Street, Pasquin's Street, Place Navona, Pantheon's Place, Place of the Column, and through the length of the Corso. We had very good seats in the Square, and minute after minute some report of how the slow show was winding on its way. A man was run over, and killed opposite a pork butcher's shop, and another incident was that of a lame man, lame from his youth, recovering the use of his leg, *through prayer of Guido*, as he glanced that way. The crowd crammed the man's hat with coin. So you see that the excitement was kept up all the way to the scaffold. Guido was the last to mount the scaffold-steps, he being the worst criminal. We hardly noticed or cared how the peasants died. We were all eyes and ears for Guido, as he harangued the multitude beneath. He begged forgiveness of God, and a fair construction of his act from men, and that a *Pater* and an *Ave*, with the hymn, *Salve Regina Coeli*, might be said for him. Then he turned to the Confessor, crossed and reconciled himself with decency, looking across to St. Mary's opposite, where is shown in shrine to-day a blessed and unique relic, then he rose up, briskly, then knelt down again, bent his head, adapted his neck and with the name of " *Jesus* " on his lips, received the fatal blow.

The headsman showed the head to the populace ; I must own that I—and my friends—were disappointed in the face of the head ! It was no face to please a wife ! Report had it that he was fully six feet high, youngish, considering his fifty years, but that's report ! His friends say that his costume was at fault : he wore the dress he did the murder in, russet serge dress, black camisole, coarse cloak of baracan, white hat and cotton cap beneath, poor Count, preservative against the

N

evening dews during the journey from Arezzo. Well, so died the man and so his end was peace ; whence many a moral were to meditate.—"

I take my book, this old yellow volume and toss it once more. . . . I shall be lonely when I lay it down, it has been my four years intimate !—Thanks to the care of Cencini, the Florentine, I find, discreetly bound within its covers, the whole position of the case, pleading and summary, with three letters to the point.   I look at the first and see the actual sand, that dried the ink, not rubbed away, though written the day its writer told the deed.

It is a letter by Don Giacinto Arcangeli, to his friend and fellow advocate Cencini.   It begins that the world may read ; its writer's self is in the postscript—meant only for the eye of his friend.

The latter tells that Cencini's justificative points arrived too late to benefit Count Guido Franceschini now with God.   Arcangeli sets forth how the Court of the Governor having found Guido and his associates guilty, he, Arcangeli, after expending great effort and pains, obtained a respite and leave to claim and prove exemption from the law's award, by alleging the power and privilege of the clericate, to which effect a courier was despatched but e'er the answer came from Arezzo the Pope had dispensed with the claim of " privilege " and signed the death warrant for Guido and the four, refusing even to consider the plea of tender age put forth for Pasquini, one of the accomplices.   Always with his eye on the family and friends of the late Count, Arcangeli thus describes his end " So that all five, to-day, have suffered death with no distinction save in dying,—he, decollated by way of privilege, the rest hanged, decently and in order.   Thus came the Count to his end of gallant man, defunct in faith and exemplarity ; nor shall the shield of his great house lose shine, nor its blue banner blush to red thereby."

The true man Arcangeli, other than advocate looking

to his future prospects, peeps out of the postscript.

" There, old fox, show the clients t'other side
And keep this corner sacred, I beseech ! "

He tells him that his " aid " came too late, but even
had it been in time and Guido able to plead twenty
clericates of what avail would it have been when the
thick head of the Pope was only to be satisfied by seeing
Guido's drop into the bag ? He says " How these old
men like giving youth a push ! " He condoles with
himself that his " superb defence " had been of so
little good, but argues that his substantial arguments
will remain on record, while the Pope's ineptitude and
obstinacy will accompany him to the tomb ; he adds
" What do I care how soon ? " He is sure that thinking Rome will see and understand ? " Rome will have
relished heartily the show, yet understood the motives,
never fear, . . . and recognise the spite and the
feebleness of the aged Pope."

He then changes the subject, and introduces the
son, whom he cannot keep out of his letters : " My
boy, your godson, fat-chaps Hyacinth enjoyed the
sight "—while his father was plodding in his study.
It was a promise given to the child that if Arcangeli
failed to save Guido's head he, the little lad, should see
it chopped off ! " While my boy was seated in the box,
all eyes and ears for the show, folks chatted. One said
to him ' This time, you see, Bottini rules the roast, nor
could your father with all his eloquence, save Guido.'
The boy pouted, was quiet a moment, then rapped out
his answer, pretty smart too for an impromptu, ' Papa
knew better than aggrieve his Pope, and baulk him of
his grudge against our Count, else he'd have argued
off Bottini's ' . . . what ? ' his nose ! '—wasn't that
clever ? . . . I can tell you he's a boy to be proud of.
He's only eight and out of Caesar, and it would be
difficult to catch him tripping in Eutropius. He's an
incentive to me to strain every nerve to do him justice !
I'll make him a great lawyer and as dual-fine an orator

as old Bartolus-cum-Baldo. For that, purse I the pieces and take up every case of standing that I can get. When I make my call on Bottini to compliment him on confuting me, I'm pretty sure he'll answer me with grace that will own ' could eloquence avail to gainsay fact yours were the victory, be comforted ! ' —I mean my little Cinuzzo to be gainer by it all— So be proud of your godson ! "

The third letter bound in book is from Bottini, Fisc, to no matter whom. It is written on a Monday two days after the execution. The gist of it is that truth has been at issue with a lie, and gained the day, by his, Bottini's eloquence and prowess ! He writes, " Well, it is over, ends as I foresaw."

> " Easily proved, Pompilia's innocence !
> Catch them entrusting Guido's guilt to me !
> I had, as usual, the plain truth to plead."

Describes, how Guido showed what a poltroon he was, at the first twist of the cord, by turning white, and also by fully confessing his crime and dying a penitent. Bottini imagines Arcangeli, his rival, clapping his wings, and crowing that in spite of the formidable facts he had had to face, he had kept the Fisc a whole month at bay, and if it had not been for the perversity of the Pope, had foiled him of the prize!—All the same, says Bottini, any skill, any work really done in defence of Guido, was due to Spreti " mannikin and dandiprat mere candle-end and inch of cleverness stuck on Arcangeli's save-all, that he is."—I knew that Arcangeli would grin and brag, but what I was *not* prepared for, was the downright audacity, impudence, impertinence of that barefoot Augustinian, that monk, whose report of the dying woman's words did detriment to my best points it took the freshness from. That meddler preached at San Lorenzo, yesterday, as a winding-up o' the shows—which have proved a treasure to the Church—He took for his text " Let God be true, and every man a liar." What he said on his text I can

best report by sending you the longest-winded of the
paragraphs. . . . The sermon has been printed and
posts through Rome to-day. You and I must engage
never to forget this man's shameless application and his
crass action. You will find that this one paragraph
runs into close on two thousand words, and already it
has had such an effect that one of my clients who had
intended to appeal from the absurd decision of the
Court, has now gone back on his intention and says
that so far as he cares " the liars may possess the
world," that he'll not call on lawyers' help any more.
So may I whistle for my job and fee ! But just read
that part of the sermon I've enclosed. The heart of it
is this :—" Suppose you that because you have seen
truth triumph, and Pompilia's purity prevail, that *all*
Truth triumphs in the end ? So might the old dwellers
in the ark have argued that because the dove returned
safely there had been no danger all the while o' the
deluge to any other winged things ! Then he continues
" Methinks I hear the Patriarch's warning voice—

> " Though this one breast, by miracle, return,
> No wave rolls by, in all the waste, but bears
> Within it some dead dove-like thing as dear,
> Beauty made blank and harmlessness destroyed ! "

Pertinent is the question he asks and one likely to
appeal to the crowd—the people—he says " How many
chaste and noble sister-fames

> Wanted the extricating hand, and lie
> Strangled, for one Pompilia, proud above
> The welter, plucked from the world's calumny,
> Stupidity, simplicity,—who cares ? "

You can gauge how this kind of sentiment will find its
answer and mislead thousands of the people. But this
was not the worst of the monk's statements. His
temerity hesitated not to hold up law to ridicule and
contempt. After showing how circumstances gathering
like clouds, obscured Pompilia's fame—" pearl-pure "
—as he phrased it, he bade the people note how the
obscurity became eclipse by " *The inadequacy and*

ineptitude of law."   Here are his words on the subject,
you'll read them in their setting in the extract I've
sent you.

> " Hear law, appointed to defend the just,
> Submit, for best defence, that wickedness
> Was bred of flesh and innate with the bone
> Borne by Pompilia's spirit for a space,
> And no mere chance fault, passionate and brief " :

The entire sermon was reprehensible ; both high and low
are attacked.   If that were not so he would certainly
have the sentence of his text thus : " God is true and
every man a liar *save the Pope, happily reigning.*"—

I'll teach the rabid, impudent monk if law be " in-
adequate and impotent," and luck is on my side—he'd
call it " Providence " were it on his—for the Monastery
of the Convertites, where the Court consigned Pompilia
first, claims every paul of every sinner that dies within
its walls.   Now Pompilia devised all the wealth of the
old couple, which by their death devolved on her, in
trust for her son and heir Gaetano—trust to end with
infancy, but she made a leading mistake as law will
show our friend, the monk.   The Court found Guido
guilty, but pronounced no word about the innocency
of his wife : Pompilia was unrelieved by formal sentence from the fault imputed to her, and was therefore
unfit and unable to dispose of her property, which,
therefore, became the property of the Monastery.
Isn't this clear as the eye of day ? My next task will
be to prove Pompilia, whom last week I sainted so,
a person of dishonest life ! and so *I'll* teach the *monk*
what Scripture means, and that the tongue should
prove a two-edged sword,— . . .

> " No adequate machinery in law ?
> No power of life and death in the learned tongue ? "

Why I can fancy myself already at my speech, startling
the world with " Thou Pompilia, thus ? How is the
fine gold of the Temple dim ! "—and so forth.
But I, Robert Browning, two hundred years later

cry " Alack Bottini, my little old yellow book tells of
thy defeated plans and shows an Instrument, dated
September of the same year in which justice was
wrought on Guido and his four.   The old Pope was
yet living then.   Here are the words of the Instrument : " In restitution of the perfect fame of dead
Pompilia, *quondam* Guido's wife, and warrant to her
representative

> Domenico Tighetti, barred hereby,
> While doing duty in his guardianship
> From all molesting, all disquietude,
> Each perturbation and vexation brought
> Or threatened to be brought against the heir
> By the Most Venerable Convent called
> Saint Mary Magdalen o' the Convertites
> I' the Corso "

So justice was done a second time !   The *locum
tenens* for the Governor at the time was one whose
name I have added last to my list, wishing to preserve
it, as its owner gave effect to the Instrument.

My Pope—Innocent XII.,—died the next year but
one—completing his nine years of rule in Rome ; some
say he died on his accession day.   If he thought
doubt would do the next age good it's a pity that he
died unapprised of the birth of *Voltaire.*   And so with
the death of my Pope ends the story.   I can find no
record of Pompilia's child grown to man.

> " Our Gaetano, born of love and hate
> Did the babe live or die ? . . .
> What were his fancies if he grew a man ?
> Was he proud . . . of bearing blasoned arms,
> Or did he love his mother, the base born,
> And fight in the ranks, unnoticed by the world ? "

Guido's sister, Porzia, I find by a record in the annals
of the town of Arezzo, moved the Priors of Arezzo and
their head to give a public attestation to the right of
Franceschini to men's reverence—apparently because
of the incident of the murder.—Here is the translation
of nearly the " worst Latin ever writ."

" Since antique time whereof the memory
Holds the beginning, to this present hour,
Our Franceschini ever shone, and shine,
Still i' the primary rank, supreme amid
The lustres of Arezzo, proud to own
In this great family—her flag-bearer,
Guide of her steps and guardian against foe,—
As in the first beginning so to-day ! "

There now, after that statement do you still maintain that *History* is to be trusted before the insight of a poet ?

Look at that phrase " Supreme amid the lustres of Arezzo."—Are Petrarch, and Michael Angelo less worthy than —Guido— ? Was Livy only mirthful when he ascribed the foundation of Arezzo to Janus, the *Double-Face* ?

So, British Public, who may like me yet, my story, —the transmutation of the facts of the old yellow book,—teaches, or offers you one lesson : This :—

That our human speech is naught,
Our human testimony false, our fame
And human estimation words and wind.

Do you ask me why take this trouble, the artistic way to prove so much ? My answer is because it is the glory and good of Art, the one way possible of speaking the truth to mankind. . . . Art may tell a truth obliquely, do the thing shall breed the thought, nor wrong the thought, missing the mediate word. Painters, musicians, authors may show double truth, bring music from the mind, open and suffice the eye while saving the soul.

" And save the soul ! If this intent save mine—
If the rough ore be rounded to a ring,
Render all duty which good ring should do,
And, failing grace, succeed in guardianship,—
Might mine but lie outside thine, Lyric Love,
Thy rare gold ring of verse (the poet[1] praised)
Linking our England to his Italy ! "

[1] Tommaso Tommasei wrote an inscription for the Casa Guidi Tablet "Here wrote and died Elizabeth Barrett Browning . . . . who made of her verse a golden ring linking Italy and England."